Your Next Role

D0309998

Your Next Role

Role

How to get ahead and get promoted

Niamh O'Keeffe

PEARSON

Harlow, England • London • New York • Boston • San Francisco • Toronto • Sydney
Auckland • Singapore • Hong Kong • Tokyo • Seoul • Taipei • New Delhi
Cape Town • São Paulo • Mexico City • Madrid • Amsterdam • Munich • Paris • Milan

Pearson Education Limited
Edinburgh Gate
Harlow CM20 2JE
United Kingdom
Tel: +44 (0)1279 623623

Web: www.pearson.com/uk

First published 2016 (print and electronic)

© Niamh O'Keeffe 2016 (print and electronic)

The right of Niamh O'Keeffe to be identified as author of this work has been asserted by her in accordance with the Copyright, Designs and Patents Act 1988.

ISBN: 978–1-292–11250–3 (print)
     978–1-292–11252–7 (PDF)
     978–1-292–11253–4 (ePub)

British Library Cataloguing-in-Publication Data
A catalogue record for the print edition is available from the British Library

Library of Congress Cataloging-in-Publication Data
A catalog record for the print edition is available from the Library of Congress

10 9 8 7 6 5 4 3 2 1
20 19 18 17 16

Cover design by Dan Mogford
Print edition typeset in 11/14pt Frutiger LT Com by Lumina Datamatics
Printed by Ashford Colour Press Ltd, Gosport

NOTE THAT ANY PAGE CROSS REFERENCES REFER TO THE PRINT EDITION

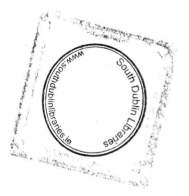

I would like to dedicate this book to my daughter Meera.

Contents

About the author

Niamh O'Keeffe is a leadership consultant and provides advice to corporate executives on how to be a great leader. Niamh offers a unique approach, rooted in what she calls 'The Leadership Lifecycle'. The lifecycle approach takes a strategic view of the whole leadership role challenge chunked into critical time and outcome-based phases: how to get a leadership role, how to have a positive beginning, how to stay the course, when and how to leave the role constructively in order to move on to the next challenge.

With a career track record of 23 years, including 8 years with Accenture as a strategy consultant and 2 years as an executive search consultant in the city of London, Niamh O'Keeffe is also the founder of First100 www.First100assist.com and a twice-published author with Pearson.

Since 2004, Niamh's leadership consultancy work with First100 focused on advising senior executives on how to have a successful first 100 days in a new leadership role appointment. Those advisory services led her organically into working with clients on the pre-first-100-days stage of how to get a leadership promotion. This book, *Your Next Role: how to get ahead and get promoted*, is the most recent addition to Niamh's book series with Pearson and represents the prequel to her two books on the topic of 'Your First 100 Days'.

Your First 100 Days: how to make maximum impact in your new leadership role (published 2011 by FT Publishing; translated into Spanish, Chinese, Japanese and Korean).

Lead your Team in your First 100 Days (published 2013 by FT Publishing; widely used as a management training resource).

Acknowledgements

Thanks to Colm Flood for running the interviews process, writing up the case studies and gathering executive quotes. Thanks to Eimee Kuah for her advice and encouragement. A special acknowledgement to John O'Keeffe for his helpful contributions and timely critiques. Finally, I would like to thank my editor, David Crosby, from Pearson for his support and patience.

Publisher's acknowledgements

We are grateful to the following for permission to reproduce copyright material:

Quote on p.53 from Ariel Eckstein as Managing Director, LinkedIn EMEA.; Quote on p.53 from Jane Griffiths from Janssen, the pharmaceutical companies of Johnson & Johnson; Quote on p.54 from Stephen Frost as Visiting Fellow at Harvard University & Head of Diversity and Inclusion, KPMG; Quote on p.58 from Vimi Grewal-Carr as Managing Partner for Innovation and Delivery Models, Deloitte Consulting; Quote on p.58 from Mai Fyfield as Chief Strategy Officer, Sky; Quote on p.59 from Peter Skodny as Country Managing Director, Accenture; Quote on p.59 from Ian Powell as Chairman and Senior Partner at PwC; Quote on p.58 from Colum Honan as Consultant, Expense Reduction Analysts (UK) Ltd; Quote on p.63 from Gareth McWilliams as General Manager Operations, BT Business / SME; Quote on p.87 from Bill Archer as Managing Director, Eir Business; Quote on p.87 from David Hulsenbek as Head of Human Resources, ABN AMRO Private Banking International; Quote on p.88 from Jacqueline McNamee as Managing Director UK, AIG; Quote on p.88 from

John Harker as Chief Human Resources Officer, Al-Futtaim; Quote on p.100 from Ariel Eckstein as Managing Director, LinkedIn; Quote on p.103 from Michael Kleef as Director of Audience Marketing, Microsoft; Quote on p.120 from Dr Angel Gavieiro as SVP, Financial Services; Quote on p.120 from Laurie Bowen as Chief Executive Officer Business Solutions, Cable & Wireless Communications; Quote on p.125 from Jens Backes as Vice President, Access Services, Telecoms Industry; Quote on p.125 from Joan Hogan as Group Senior Manager, Technology Industry (Microsoft.com); Quote on p.125 from Peter Rawlinson as Chief Marketing Officer, Continuity Control; Quote on p.126 from Georgina Farrell as Head of HR UK Insurance, Multi-national; Quote on p.126 from Marcus Millership as Head of Human Resources, Rolls Royce Shared Services; Quote on p.132 from Andrew Farmer as CIO International Financial Services, Commonwealth Bank of Australia; Quote on p.132 from Avril Twomey as Head of Marketing, Glenilen Farm; Quote on p.139 from Andrea Guerzoni as Transaction Advisory Services Leader for Europe, Middle East, India and Africa (EMEIA) EY; Quotes on p.141, p.162 from John Quinn as Group Chief technology Officer, Digicel; Quote on p.146 from Jan Zijderveld as President of Unilever, Europe; Quote on p.161 from Darren Price as Group Chief Information Officer and Executive Board Member, RSA Insurance Group; Quote on p.163 from Carl Fitzsimons as Group HR Director, Thai Union.

Introduction

- Who should read this book?
- What you will learn
- Follow my advice and get promoted

Who should read this book?

This book has relevance to anybody with ambition and leadership potential who wants to invest in their upward career trajectory. The promotion formula in this book can be utilised by anyone who is willing to work smart. It can be applied to any rung of the career ladder, and suits every level of leadership.

The target readership of this book are people at junior and middle-management level in corporations, and any other more senior level of executive who feels stuck on their particular rung of the promotional ladder. This book is for those who want to get promoted faster and seek to find some answers and a fresh edge to get ahead. These are the ambitious employees who want to fulfil their potential, but may find that while they have successfully navigated their way to their existing management position, they are now floundering as to how to work out the people and politics necessary to keep their career on an upward trajectory.

There are various target promotion scenarios:

- Juniors who aspire to move into first rung of management
- Managers who want to get promoted to Senior Manager

- Senior Managers who want to get promoted to Director
- Directors who want to get promoted to General Manager
- General Managers who want to expand their geographies or responsibilities
- Members of the Top 100 Leaders of a firm who want to get to CEO or Group CEO Level.

Although each step up may seem as if it would require separate answers, in fact my promotion formula can be applied to each of these essential leadership transitions – adjusted appropriately to your level and capability.

My clients and this book's target audience are members of global corporations, but the book has relevance for all those working in SMEs as well.

What you will learn

You may not have realised that 'how to get promoted' is an essential leadership skill. This is a useful reframe of something that perhaps you thought was just a company process. Once you see it as a skill, in its own right, then you appreciate that this is something you need to learn and apply again and again in order to navigate your way up through the corporate ranks.

My emphasis throughout the book is that you should be in charge of your own career destiny – as much as possible. Although we can't control everything, we can certainly set out a **you have more power than you think** plan for our career, adjusting it as time goes by, and control our response to what happens. You have more power than you think. You will learn how fundamentally important it is that you empower yourself and develop the confidence and courage to push boundaries.

I offer you tips and strategies on how to get outside your comfort zone in order to get promoted. You will need to build a platform of great results, navigate the politics, impress others and create your own successful future. A lot of people go wrong by ignoring the politics involved in promotion decisions. I will help you to read the organisation and gain more political astuteness. If you learn how to address the politics of your promotion, you will be better able to understand the organisation context, and better able to influence the decision-makers and stack the odds in your favour.

In the race to get promoted, you might think it very important to somehow cut down or knock out the competition. In truth, I have never found this to be true. When I work with my clients, I focus entirely on what my clients can do to improve themselves and their chances of promotion. I don't think about the competition and how to pull them down as part of the strategy. When you focus on improving your own value proposition for the role, rather than worry about the competition, then you will be better placed to succeed.

Key skills you will learn:

- An essential leadership skill unlocked: i.e. the skill of 'how to get promoted'

- Self-empowerment: more confidence on how to approach the task of getting promoted

- Political astuteness: more awareness of how to influence decision-makers, and how to deal with organisation processes, people and politics

- How to get a competitive edge: set yourself apart from your peers by improving your own value proposition and not worrying about anyone else

- Get unstuck: break free of institutionalised thinking about 'this is how it works' to create more opportunities for your promotion success.

Follow my advice and get promoted

The good news is that if you really want to get promoted, and you follow the advice in this book, you will get promoted. Most people are so busy in the detail, and so mired in their day-to-day work and life demands, that they are missing the bigger picture. I will guide you on how to step back, and take the time to think more strategically about your next role move, and back it up with tactical action, and give you an edge on everyone else.

Why am I so confident that I can help you? Because in my experience it is highly likely that you have become institutionalised into a work system that creates a 'stuckness' in your mind on how things happen. Going to university is fantastic, but it also **it is highly likely you have become institutionalised** programmes you to think in a particular way. Joining a corporate is exciting, and the first step in your career, but immediately you are 'trained' to operate within the culture and a set of norms (rules) to which your once free mind inevitably succumbs.

The norms go something like this: at the beginning, *'It will take you 5 years to become a Manager'*; and later, *'It will take you 3–5 more years to become a Senior Manager.'* Then, as the years go by, the confident statements drop off to become more vague and insecure like, *'Well, it's a pyramid structure and not everyone can make it.'* *'Do well in this role, and who knows.'* And then more years go by, with no real plan and no one – least of all you – taking charge of your career. The more years of experience you have in the corporate system, the more stuck you have become in thinking *'this is the way it works'*. Now and again, a peer, or worse still, a former junior, leaps ahead. This disturbs your status quo. How did that happen? I am better than that guy, so why did she or he get that role?

Your peace of mind is disturbed, and so it should be. Let me be the catalyst to get you out of your comfort zone, to get you to really feel your discomfort at others whizzing past you in the career trajectory.

By freeing you of any stuck thoughts, and getting you to feel your disturbance, I can liberate you to achieve what you want. You don't need to wait and wait to get what you want; you just need to focus and open yourself up to take on the challenge.

Commit

- Get ready to do the work
- Consider why you are not already promoted
- How not to get promoted: Top 10 mistakes
- Commit to a new beginning

1 Get ready to do the work

You bought this book because you want to get promoted. Who wouldn't want a pay rise, a better and more exciting role, an opportunity to climb the career ladder and fulfil their leadership potential? But the first point I make to each of my executive coaching clients, and now I need to make it to you, is that you might under-appreciate the extent to which you will likely need to mature and change. Everyone wants a quick fix solution to a pressing need. You may

you bought this book because you want to get promoted

find some top tips and quick fixes leap off these pages that work for you immediately. On the other hand, if it's deep learning you want, on how to secure leadership promotion after promotion, all the way to the top, it's all in here for you – but get ready to do the work!

When I say 'the work' I mean more than your on-the-job performance. Naturally you will need to deliver good results in your day job to prove you can get to the next level. But what I really mean by 'the work' is the total sum of energy and effort that it takes to get the promotion. As well as establishing an impressive platform of current role results, you will need to

learn how to navigate the politics and manage your stakeholders

learn how to navigate the politics and manage your stakeholders, and have the confidence and resilience to keep moving forward in spite of any discouragement or unforeseen obstacles. As you will soon learn from the Get-Promoted Framework, getting promoted is about a lot more than just achieving on your current role targets and deliverables. If anything, I want you to rebalance your time in your current job, by working smarter and getting your team and others to step up for you, while you create more space to do what is needed to secure your promotion. As you empower yourself and empower others, it will be a win for you, your team and the organisation.

With one senior client, all it took for me to get him promoted was a 45-minute conversation advising him on what he needed to say to his boss. Within a few weeks his boss was on board, and within a few months he was formally promoted from ordinary partner level to Chief Operating Officer of his firm. His next promotion was significantly harder to achieve because it required a great deal more work from him in terms of raising his confidence levels, and his true commitment to working harder to make another leadership step-up. In another case, it took 18 months for a new client to apply my advice and really change her approach – but when she did, she leapfrogged her peers and was promoted straight into a role on the CEO's management team. In another case, my client wanted a promotion but wasn't prepared to put much work in at all, and while he made the longlist from manager to director promotion, unfortunately he didn't fulfil enough of their criteria to get shortlisted or selected.

So there is the advice, and then there is what you are going to do with that advice. It's up to you to take what you want from the book, but the more open you are to learn and change, the faster you will get promoted.

YOU WILL NEED WILL AS WELL AS WANT

When the decision-makers consider who to promote, very often it comes down to not just skill, but 'will' as well. They ask themselves: '*Does this person*

it comes down to not just skill, but 'will'

have a "will" for the role, i.e. how much does he really want it? Because if he really wants it, he will work harder to make a success of the role and I feel more comfortable appointing him above the other guy who may be more qualified but doesn't seem as passionate or convincing.'

We all procrastinate or get a bit lazy when it comes to putting in maximum effort, unless we feel really motivated. As you will see from the diagnostic section coming up next, you may have to face some painful realisations about yourself and your environment and why you are not already promoted for three or more years. I map out all the possibilities so that you will have a greater awareness on the gap areas, and how you may need to change. It may start to feel like hard work, and you may not feel like putting in the effort to address the gaps. Or, worse still, perhaps you are already so disinclined to do the work that you start to flick through the pages of the diagnostic, without really taking the appropriate time to seriously think and explore reasons why you are not yet promoted. It's no problem if you don't want to do the work. Just don't expect a promotion as well! That is a recipe for disappointment – all of your own creation.

Sorry for being so serious. Perhaps, for many of you, I am just exaggerating to make the point. In any case, I am prepping you for what is ahead so that I can help you, and we can move forward faster on getting you that promotion, and the next one and the next one. The more you learn about what you lack, the faster you can work on resolving your issues and the closer you will get to that promotion. Although it sounds counterintuitive, the more we can flush out your issues, and get them all on the table, the more confident you will become. There will be a sense of relief from having a greater understanding of yourself and your challenges, and then the real work can begin.

The competition for promotion from middle ranks to the top table is fierce, even if not overt – or should I say *especially* if it is not overt, because hidden politics and agendas are even harder to navigate. Getting promoted takes energy and focus. Naturally you want the promotion, but commitment to a promotion is about making a promise to yourself that not only do you want the promotion, but that you have the will for it.

- How much do you really want the promotion?
- Are you ready to grow and change?
- Are you willing to take risks?
- Can you move outside your comfort zone?
- Are you easily discouraged, or can you get excited by the prospect of what it takes?

PERHAPS YOU CAN'T AFFORD NOT TO GET PROMOTED

The trouble with corporate life is that deciding not to invest in getting promoted is problematic too. If you are not demonstrating sufficient ambition compared with your peers, you may be seen as just coasting, and you might eventually lose your job. As you become more senior, the harder it is to get the next promotion. There are fewer roles and it takes more effort, so it might even feel easier to wait it out to see if 'they' promote you. I can tell you now that being passive is a very risky strategy. If you are not demonstrating sufficient ambition compared with peers, you are more likely to get demoted or lose your job. You are also in danger of having a mid-life, mid-career crisis later on – regretting that you never made the effort when you had the opportunity.

being passive is a very risky strategy

I worked with a senior client to successfully secure him a C-level promotion. As a member of the executive leadership team, he could have easily used that platform to subsequently pitch for the Group CEO role. However, he was lazy and also probably afraid of the demands that the top role would bring, so despite his potential he decided he didn't want to go any further forward. Guess what happened next? A new Group CEO was appointed; my guy lost his seat at the top table, and was demoted back into the rank and file of ordinary director. So think carefully about what you want, and if you're not fully in, don't be surprised if others push you back down the ranks again. I have given you a very senior example, but the same holds true at every level in the organisation. If you are not seen to be ambitious at whatever level you are, then don't be surprised if you lose your seat at the management table.

In another case, I had a very senior client who was a member of the Top 200 Leaders in a global corporation, and therefore eligible for consideration for a Top 25 job. I had to remind him that being eligible promises nothing. It is just a starting point for possibilities. My client wanted a promotion but didn't realise he had to put in the work for it. Why don't members of the Top 200 realise that the majority – possibly 175 or more – won't necessarily ever get another promotion – ever? Very often the top team of 25 monopolise the leadership team for years by rotating around the top jobs. So there is very little movement at the top, combined with constant pressure from the ranks below to join the Top 200 each year. All this means is that you reach the Top 200 and unless you DO SOMETHING WITH THAT OPPORTUNITY, you simply come off the list again within a few years. It is just the maths, but people delude themselves into thinking that because they were told they could be a Top 25 leader, this will automatically lead to exciting Top 25 leadership appointment promotions. This also holds true in the junior ranks for those of you who are part of Top Talent programmes. On being selected into Top Talent programmes in your twenties, it is all very exciting. The organisation is full of 'promises' about how this means that you have potential

being eligible promises nothing

to make CEO 'one day' and how you are on the path towards that big bright future – but in reality these high-potential development programmes often run their course within a few years, or are disbanded when cost reductions are necessary, and you may find yourself on your own again trying to navigate your own way to the top.

I want to open your eyes so that you realise that you are the one who needs to take charge of your career, and you are the one who needs to have inner drive and the self-motivation necessary to overcome obstacles to get the promotions you want. You are the one who needs to put in the work, and when you do, anything is possible. You may even become the Group CEO, if that is what you want.

So, with all that serious lecturing behind us now, if you are still up for a positive learning experience, then I have the answers for you, so read on! Don't get overwhelmed. See it all as a positive learning opportunity and a wonderful investment in your work self.

2 Consider why you are not already promoted

The promise of this book is to help you to get promoted. Let's start with a diagnosis of your current situation to find clues as to why you have not already moved up to the next level. If you work that out, you will be in a better place to figure out what you need to do next. This section is about being really honest with your work self. Take a step back and try to take as detached a perspective as possible. If you feel frustrated, don't just jump to the idea that it is the fault of others who 'misunderstand' you. Start with the default that while there may be other factors involved, it is quite likely that the diagnosis will reveal that you are the primary person getting in the way of your own promotion.

DIAGNOSE THE REASONS

Consider all possible factors within your promotional environment. Once you have diagnosed the underlying issues, you will be better placed to resolve them and fast track your path to promotion.

Table 1.1 Diagnostic

PROMOTIONAL ENVIRONMENT	WHAT IS GOING WRONG?
You	Are you getting in the way of your promotion?
Your boss	Does your boss undervalue you, or overvalue you?
Your team	If your team is not a winning team, does this affect your prospects?
Your company	Is it a very competitive company, with lots of politics to overcome?
The economy	Is the economy in recession or growth mode?

You: are you getting in the way of your promotion?

It is usually easier to blame others and external factors outside our control. However, you need to take responsibility for what you are – or are not – doing that is delaying your promotion.

The good news is that if you are the reason why you are not yet promoted, and you are committed to changing, then it should be easier to change yourself than to change others. You may find some of the observations below shallow – for example why should it matter what you wear or how you look? – but I am just making it plain for you to realise that although these things may not matter to me or you, they may well matter to the person who has the power to promote you. Consider what they value.

Table 1.2 Reasons not promoted: you

REASONS NOT PROMOTED	
Performance gap	Obviously you have to be performing well in your current role in order to be considered for the next role. Furthermore, you need to be taking on responsibilities from your boss so that you are seen to be able to operate at the level above your current role. Are you meeting your performance objectives and exceeding the expectations of your boss? Are you showing evidence of your ability to operate at the next level up? Get out your last three performance appraisals. What were the key messages? Spot the pattern of feedback on your performance gaps.
Confidence gap	If you don't think you really deserve the promotion, then no one else will either. First, you need to believe in yourself. Despite what is said, the corporation is not a meritocracy. The best people do not necessarily get promoted. Sometimes it is confidence alone that gets some people ahead. I would like to equip you to be confident, combined with developing your core strengths to get on the path to promotion.
Recognition gap	If waiting to be acknowledged for all your efforts has not resulted in a promotion, then this passive strategy is not working for you and it is time to take action.
Skill gap	Are there skills gaps that you need to bridge – e.g. strategic, leadership or technical skills? You may need to invest in further developing yourself – possibly in your own time and with your own money. If you feel you don't have the strategic or leadership experience to lead at the next level yet, there is always a coach or a training course that can bridge the gap – whether you fund it, or the company funds it.
Behaviour gap	Perhaps you are perceived to be too arrogant, too challenging or possibly too junior, or too unassertive for promotion to the next level. With an improved level of self-awareness and help from the right mentor or coach, you can correct unhelpful behaviours.

▶

REASONS NOT PROMOTED	
Interpersonal gap	An all too common reason for lack of promotion to the next leadership level occurs when the person is technically very bright, but simply lacks the required emotional intelligence and interpersonal skills to lead other people. The more likeable and popular you are, the easier it will be to promote you. At the same time, it is important that people respect you. You could be liked, but not respected – and the latter could be the reason for non-promotion.
Communication gap	Perhaps you are doing great work, but not communicating the effort or the results. This is a classic reason for people to fall victim to non-promotion. In the world of 'busy, busy' corporate land, if you don't properly showcase what you do, no one is going to take the time to discover your genius.
Image gap	Depending on your company culture and dress code, it may be hampering your chances if you are not presenting the right image. Observe how the high-performing managers and leaders present themselves in your company.
Other	Is there another reason specific to you? For example is there something about your reputation that may be an issue? Do you tend to over-promise and under-deliver? Nobody wants to promote someone who is all talk and no action. If this is you, you will need to reset your course immediately. It can be a powerful 'fresh start' strategy to let people know that you are aware of your faults and you have started to course correct.

Be honest with yourself, and write down the real reasons why you may be getting in the way of your own promotion.

Your boss: is your boss getting in the way of your promotion?

Naturally we like to blame our boss when we don't secure a promotion. It is true, of course, that they usually have the biggest input on the decision. So let's deal with why the boss is not promoting you.

Table 1.3 Reasons not promoted: your boss

REASONS NOT PROMOTED	
Undervalued by boss	If your boss doesn't rate you, ask him for specific feedback on what you lack. For example, the boss may say you are not 'strategic' enough for the next level. Don't be discouraged because with the right help you can overcome any skill gaps highlighted.
Overvalued by boss	If your boss needs you to stay because you are indispensable or needs you to continue to make him look good, or if he feels threatened by you, he is not incentivised to promote you. This happens more often than you think.
Boss has no input on promotional decision	There are cases where your boss does value you, and has put you forward for promotion, but doesn't have any input/influence over the decision. He may not want to admit that he has no influence so this has to be your judgement call. You could focus your efforts beyond your boss to build a relationship with your boss's boss, and try to find out who are the real decision-maker(s) when it comes to your promotion.
Boss values you but has not emotionally committed to getting you promoted	Your boss may value you, but has not emotionally committed to helping you to get promoted. It's your job to put him under pressure to support you. Perhaps he needs to be told by you how strongly you feel about getting promoted. He won't want an unhappy worker on his team and may feel that it is finally time to help you.

Distinguishing between when your boss undervalues you versus overvalues you will not be as easy as you may think. Even when the boss overvalues you, he may give out mixed signals in order to keep you under control, and in your place.

Set up a meeting with your boss to discuss your promotion prospects. Don't construct the question in a negative way *'Why haven't I been promoted?'* Instead ask a more confidently styled question *'What do you think it will take for me to get promoted to the next level?'* and then listen, listen, listen to what he or she says. The tricky thing about feedback is whether the person is being really honest with you – and also whether you can be really honest about what you need to hear. You don't have to take what they say at face value, unless you feel as if they really mean it. Confused??

the tricky thing about feedback is whether the person is being really honest with you

Well, it can be confusing, depending on the agenda and sincerity of your boss. The more sincere the boss, the more you can take what they say as being true. The good thing about this exercise is that you gather clues about the perception of you. Plus, if you and your boss can crystallise the one or two gap areas, then you can be more focused about what you need to address to achieve the promotion.

Another approach is to pick a moment when your boss is so relaxed that you can ask him informally what it would really take to get a promotion. He might just tell you something 'off the record' which ends up being more valuable than what is written in your formal performance appraisal.

Your team: is your team getting in the way of your promotion?

If your team is succeeding, then you can ride the crest of that success wave. However, all your teammates are thinking the same thing and the jostling for the next promotion can be intensely competitive. On the flipside, if your team is not succeeding then it is harder for you – or anyone else on that team – to explain why you could possibly deserve a promotion as a member of that team that is not performing adequately.

Table 1.4   Reasons not promoted: your team

REASONS NOT PROMOTED	
Team is succeeding	As a contributing member of a successful team, perhaps there is intense competition among teammates as everyone jostles for the few available promotions.
Team not succeeding	If you are part of a non-critical or non-winning team then it is difficult for your boss to justify promoting you. You could offer to play an instrumental role in fixing the problem and bringing the team to higher performance – and/or demonstrate added value as a good individual contributor despite the poor performance of the team.

Your company: is your company getting in the way of your promotion?

In most corporations there is usually a well-managed promotion cycle operated by Human Resources (HR) up to manager level – and after that, although there may be a 'process', it is not always clear how some make it to the next level and some don't ever get beyond being stuck in the middle ranks. This is called politics. It is an organisational reality and if you don't engage with it, you will lose out in your career.

Table 1.5   Reasons not promoted: your company

REASONS NOT PROMOTED	
Company culture	If promotions are very rare, or tenure-based, then it is harder to fast track in an institutionalised culture than in a more flexible corporate culture. For example, public service organisations may be particularly tenure-based and there is no way around it. Think about the norms in your company, and how long it takes on average to get promoted. You may have to move to a new company to get promoted faster.

▶

Power and politics	Who really makes the decision? For example, although HR may not have the power to promote you, in many corporates they almost certainly have the power to block your promotion. Keep your HR folks and any other key influencers onside. Help out HR when they need business volunteers to speak at their events, or to join one of their cross-company initiatives.
Structural sexism and unconscious bias	Structural sexism and unconscious bias may be operating at your company. Decision-makers may be unconsciously biased towards people who look like them, or went to the same school or clubs. Women or members of the LGBT (Lesbian, Gay, Bi-sexual, and Transgender) community may find it particularly difficult to get promoted in very macho and male-dominated environments. It is very difficult to change structural embedded norms, and if behaviour is unconscious all you can do is to try to surface it by building awareness through using statistics, observations and diversity initiatives. Or move to a more inclusive company.
Perceptions of your division	You may be stuck in a promotional rut simply because the division you work in is not perceived by Group HQ as a talent pool. If this is the case, you may need to take a lateral move into a division that offers more opportunity for future promotion.
Competition	Naturally not everyone can get promoted. Corporates are organised in a pyramid shape, with more workers at the junior level (doing the core work) and fewer managers in the middle (managing), and even fewer chiefs at the top (leading). Ask a recently promoted colleague, who was a peer, how she got promoted. People who have already made it will be more than willing to talk about their achievements to their juniors, and pass along their advice. This can be some of the best advice you ever get – because they know how promotions really work here, so ask for their perspectives on what they thought it would take to get promoted, but what actually worked in the end.

The economy: is the economy getting in the way of your promotion?

The world economy has taken quite a battering since 2007 and it became more about keeping your job rather than getting a promotion to the next level. 'Promotions' became about two jobs being collapsed into one, with one leader losing out and the other keeping the expanded role but not getting a pay increase. In that kind of environment, you can be excused for not getting promoted as fast as you may previously have expected. Although the world has changed, and we face a new normal of low economic growth, we are coming out of recession and you can return to more optimistic views on climbing the corporate ladder.

Table 1.6 Reasons not promoted: the economy

REASONS NOT PROMOTED	
The economy	In a recession, there may be fewer opportunities for promotion. Sometimes events really are out of our control. When the world economy collapsed, you may have needed to hang on to your current job, and wait it out. However, as the economy recovers, if you can play a value-adding role on restructuring the company, it may even be possible to create a noble platform for promotion when the economy and company performance starts to pick up.

Capture your conclusions

Make notes on your reflections to date.

PROMOTIONAL ENVIRONMENT	WHAT IS GOING WRONG?
You	Are you getting in the way of your promotion?
Your boss	Does your boss undervalue you, or overvalue you?
Your team	If your team is not a winning team, does this affect your prospects?
Your company	Is it a very competitive company, with lots of politics to overcome?
The economy	Is the economy in recession or growth mode?

Let's now also examine the 10 most common reasons why people fail to get promoted, and sense-check whether any apply to your situation.

3 How not to get promoted: Top 10 mistakes

There may be specific insights emerging from your personal diagnostic, as to why you have not yet been promoted. In general people usually make one of the following Top 10 mistakes, not realising that they are operating from the manual of how-not-to rather than the how-to approach. So, to avoid your falling foul of any of the obvious errors, here goes on the rulebook of how not to get promoted:

Table 1.7   How not to get promoted

HOW NOT TO GET PROMOTED: TOP 10 MISTAKES	✔ TICK IF TRUE
1. I am not confident I can do the role at the next level up	
2. I have no strategic vision	
3. I am unwilling to relocate	
4. I expect my work to speak for itself	

5. I annoy my boss
  – No respect for deadlines
  – Consistently over-promise and under-deliver
  – I complain, gossip or have a bad attitude
  – I publicly embarrass or am disloyal to my boss, and company who pay my wage
  – I asked my boss for promotion when he was in a bad mood
  – I asked for promotion just because someone else got promoted	

6. I get defensive when I hear constructive feedback	

▶

HOW NOT TO GET PROMOTED: TOP 10 MISTAKES	✔ TICK IF TRUE
7. From time to time, I threaten to leave	
8. I am not adding any value above and beyond my current role requirements	
9. I have not expanded my skills or breadth of experience for 12 months or more	

10. I am not popular among my peers and others
  – I am difficult to deal with interpersonally
  – I am overly political and not trusted by all
  – I have questionable ethics/past conflicts and scandals	

If you have ticked any of these boxes, all hope is not lost! You can recover from any situation. It just depends on how willing you are to take responsibility for your **you can recover from any situation** behaviour and truly change to redeem yourself. Action speaks louder than words, so if any of the above resonated with you, ask yourself what action you could take to rectify the situation.

If you are not confident you can do the job at next level up

I said in the diagnostic that you may be the one getting in the way of your own promotion. In my experience, at the heart of most issues with managers and leaders, when it comes to promotion, is confidence. We are all insecure at times, but perhaps no one more so than the over-achieving corporate manager or executive. *'Am I really good enough?'* he keeps asking himself. This is why my promotion formula specifically addresses the importance of having the confidence in your ability to do the next role. Getting the promotion may be all down to your core confidence and how you project that confidence to the decision-makers.

If you have no strategic vision

Have you ever heard the words *'You are not strategic enough'*? Sometimes when a client hires me, he has heard these words from his boss as to the reason why he has not yet been promoted. Often, my client doesn't understand what this means, and how to address it. When someone says you are not strategic enough, what they mean is that you only see the detail of what is immediately ahead of you, and you are not thinking about more long-term horizons, a bigger perspective and more creative solutions. To train yourself to think more strategically, imagine that you are the CEO of the company – and think about what kinds of opportunities and concerns are facing the top leadership team. Rise above the detail of your immediate role and start to think and talk about what needs to be done by the company within three to five years. Then within that context take a more strategic approach to what you want to achieve in your role and have those types of discussions with your boss. Pepper the conversation with phrases like 'our CEO's agenda', 'over the longer-term horizon', 'what is our three-year vision', 'let's step back and see the bigger picture', and – of course! – 'how can we take a more strategic approach to resolving this problem'.

If you are unwilling to relocate

A tough choice can be the 'willingness to relocate'. Obviously this is a challenge if you have put down roots, such as children going to school already. I would urge you to do international rotations early on in your career – in your twenties and early thirties. However, if you want to go further in your career, you need to be open to relocating the family at any time. Getting to the top of a global corporation will likely mean relocation roles from time to time as your family grows up. There is nothing necessarily wrong with uprooting your family. As well as financial rewards, the many positives may include the confidence and experience your children will likely gain from international schooling and absorbing other cultures. It all comes down to your mindset and how you frame it, and if you are willing to view the rotation as an amazing experience opportunity for all the family.

RUSSELL AND HOW HE RELOCATED TO GET AHEAD

Russell was working as a senior manager in an American multinational pharmaceutical company in England. He had enjoyed a relatively fast career trajectory throughout his twenties. He had joined the company as an engineer and had been promoted to manager and then senior manager all within the space of five years. But by his early thirties, his career appeared to plateau.

Russell was performing extremely well and exceeding his deliverables. In fact, he had initiated two high-impact projects in the business – one of which had resulted in a 50% decrease in direct labour costs in the company's manufacturing plants. He received a lot of praise for these projects which gave him exposure to the Country Managing Director (CMD) and country leadership team, but he was still relatively unknown in the company headquarters in the US where decisions about promotions were signed off.

Russell realised that the only way to get the necessary exposure for promotion was to work at headquarters in the US. This was a bit of a problem for Russell. He had a young family and his wife preferred to raise the children in the UK. He could either move to a new company or perhaps try to get a short-term job at the company headquarters in the US.

At their next meeting, Russell mentioned to the CMD that he was interested in working for a year or two at the headquarters in the US. Russell also reached out to junior colleagues in the US and asked them to let him know if they heard about any opportunities. Meanwhile, he also started looking at job opportunities in other pharmaceutical companies. About three months later, the CMD got back to Russell and told him about a Research & Development Senior Manager role that was being advertised in the US company headquarters. It wasn't a promotion, but there was plenty of scope for development. On top of this, the CMD told him it would be very useful politically to have someone representing the UK voice in the role.

The CMD explained that the UK was isolated from company headquarters. This, of course, was something Russell already knew. The CMD felt he had to constantly visit the US to remind them about operations in the UK. Russell recognised that this was his opportunity and discussed his terms with the CMD. Because of the need to solve the UK isolation issue, Russell felt he had leverage and told his CMD that he would go for the role, but only if he got a pay rise and a more senior title. In addition he made it clear that this was not a permanent move – he wanted to return to the UK with his family within two years. The CMD agreed and committed to supporting Russell, and persuaded his own boss, the EMEA MD, to support Russell's appointment. Russell was appointed Director of Research & Development and relocated with his family to America.

Eighteen months later, Russell had substantially increased his network in the US company headquarters, was on first name terms with the EMEA MD, the COO and had presented three times to members of the top leadership team. He also worked closely with the CMD in the UK on raising the profile of operations in the UK at the company headquarters in the US. Within two years of leaving the UK, Russell moved back to the UK to take up the role of Country COO.

Within two years Russell had make a successful leap forward in his career from Senior Manager to Country COO because he was prepared to relocate and negotiate opportunities to progress faster.

If you expect your work to speak for itself

Commonly considered a female mistake, this is when a person thinks that all they have to do is work hard and their hard work will be recognised. Not true. Your work will not speak for itself. You need to speak up about your work. Take opportunities to present your work at team meetings, or cross-company briefings. If there are no opportunities, then create them by presenting the reasons to the agenda holder as to why it would benefit all parties to get an update on what you do.

you need to speak up about your work

If you annoy your boss

The best way not to get a promotion is to consistently annoy your boss – through your bad behaviour, bad attitude or bad practices. Sometimes it is not about being 'bad' but instead is a misalignment between you and your boss about what is important. Something as simple as poor time-keeping and being consistently 20 minutes late starting work could be upsetting your boss. It could be leading to negative associations such as you don't care about your job; you are not making an effort. Try to work out what your boss values, and mirror those behaviours where it makes sense. Don't foolishly hamper your chances, by gossiping or being disloyal or irritating your boss in any way. There is no value to be gained by annoying your boss.

If you get defensive when you hear constructive feedback

When someone gives you feedback, treat it like a gift. You can either accept it or reject it, but first try to appreciate it. Always thank the person and ask for time to think about it, whether you initially agree or disagree with what was offered. Then do take the time to think about the feedback. Is there any

when someone gives you feedback, treat it like a gift

merit in what was said? Perhaps this person has done you the greatest service by pointing out a reality, a blind spot or even a perception. Now you have more information on how others view you – rightly or wrongly. If there is a perception of you out there that isn't accurate, then don't play the victim. It's up to you to correct the perception and sort yourself out in relation to any constructive feedback.

If, from time to time, you threaten to leave

When some high-performing executives get very stressed, they routinely threaten to leave. I had a client who handed in his resignation every couple of months, usually when organisation politics overwhelmed him. His boss knew how to handle him – and how to calm him down again – but these kinds of tantrums are quite childish and everyone knows it. If you act like you always have one foot out the door, then why would the organisation ever feel secure about investing in you long term? Far from being an empowering strategy, which is probably your intent, there will come a time when they decide that these are empty threats – which makes you look weak – or that you cannot be counted on to stay – which builds distrust. You are probably looking for validation of your worth to the business, but instead you run the risk of being labelled as 'immature', a tag that will be hard to shed from organisational memory in the future.

If you are not adding any value beyond your current role description

If you want to stay in your role, continue to stay in your role. If you want a promotion, expand your role to include extra responsibilities. Ask your boss what else you can help with. Bring new ideas to the table. Continue to prove your worth in your role and push the boundaries to show you are capable of more. Think about what you can do to add value above and beyond what would ordinarily be expected from someone in your role.

If you have not expanded your skills or experience in the past 12 months or more

If you are not learning, you are stagnating, or worse you are declining while all your peer competitors continue to skill up for success. If you want a promotion, you can't be complacent about it. Other people want that promotion too. So keep learning and growing, and be fit for purpose when the next promotion round comes up. Sign up for appropriate education and leadership development courses. If your company is unwilling to invest in you, then invest in yourself using your own resources. The return on investment will be worth it in the longer term.

If you are not a popular choice

Popularity goes a long way. So does dislikeability. I always say that, in the end, organisations are highly interpersonal places; the person who is chosen for promotion has to be someone who can influence. You can try to influence with fear, but that won't suit every context and eventually your colleagues or those who fear you will find a way to pull you down. Being popular does not mean you have to be the archetype of a charming charismatic extrovert leader. 'Popular' in this context just means you need to be someone that others trust, and would be happy to work for.

4 Commit to a new beginning

Having immersed yourself in the diagnostic, and sense-checked your approach against the Top 10 mistakes of how not to get promoted, take the time now to reflect and note your findings:

- What surprised you? Surprises/good and surprises/bad.

- What were the patterns?

- Did any new insights emerge?

- What are your summary conclusions on the issue areas, and how do you need to tackle them?

CAPTURE YOUR CONCLUSIONS	
Top 5 Reasons why I am probably not yet promoted	Notes on what actions I can take

COMMIT TO A NEW BEGINNING

The 'unpromoted for three or more years' are usually – understandably – a particularly defensive bunch. In most organisations the manager population are tasked with all the heavy lifting and meeting the critical deadlines. Promotional prospects are dangled in front of them as incentive, but years can go by without any promotion materialising. The 'squeezed middle' are under immense pressure from their bosses, who are good at delegating. They are usually not properly resourced with sufficient talent or numbers on their teams and so often have to personally step in to fill the resource gaps. You may also feel lingering resentment about former peers jumping ahead, or angry that you have not yet been plucked out for promotion, or that it is unfair that you need to convince others of your obvious worth. If this is you, I get it. But you have to change your attitude if you want to get beyond the middle, and get that promotion.

The main problem I come across is with managers who feel entitled to a promotion based on their own imagined criteria – which may have little or nothing to do with company reasons for awarding more senior promotions. I understand their confusion. Becoming a manager was about doing well in their role, and getting promoted to manager was a reward for all the hard work. However, after the standard promotion track to manager, the rules change but are rarely understood or communicated as explicitly as set out in Table 1.8:

Table 1.8 Promotion myths debunked

'I work hard, so I deserve the promotion'	<u>Reality check:</u> You are supposed to work hard, that is your job and that is what you are paid to do now. It does not mean you are worthy of promotion to the next level.
'It has been three years since I was last promoted. I am due a promotion now'	<u>Reality check:</u> Unless it is stated policy, time served doesn't mean you automatically get a promotion. This is an outdated idea.
'I am a great manager. I should be promoted'	<u>Reality check:</u> Lots of people are great managers. Lots of people will stay great managers. How will you set yourself apart from the rest to demonstrate your leadership potential?
'I am on a talent list, so I will get promoted anyway'	<u>Reality check:</u> Being assigned to a talent list may work at junior levels in terms of role opportunities, up to middle management, but it is too risky a strategy to rely on these HR succession lists for senior promotions. Very often role succession lists are a paper exercise, and get trumped by decision-makers in the heat of the moment of having to decide who replaces whom, given a particular context.
'I don't care if I get it or not' 'I don't need the money'	This is the all-time greatest defence mechanism of corporate folks who don't want to put the work in. What they are really saying is 'I don't want to make the effort'. If this is you, then fine, accept it and get on with your career at the level you are at – but don't play victim at the same time. It's your choice to decide if you want to put the effort in or not.

My advice is to leave your negative baggage behind now, and commit to a fresh new start. Feeling aggrieved, resentful and angry is not going to help your case. Decision-makers want to promote buoyant, optimistic people, with leadership potential, who will come to the role with an enthusiasm and positivity for the task and challenges ahead.

leave your negative baggage behind now, and commit to a fresh new start

I had a senior manager client who constantly nagged and complained about why he wasn't yet promoted. It was off-putting to his superiors because it sounded as if he had a grievance versus a true drive and energy to get to the next level for the benefit of all concerned. Don't be a whinge! It's not a winning strategy for promotion.

Start afresh, with positivity, and convert any feelings of unfairness into a constructive determination to do the work to get that promotion. You don't need to wait for the promotion to happen to have a new beginning. Commit to a new beginning now. With a greater sense of what you want from your work life, and having worked out your career game plan, then today is an opportunity for a fresh start and a new sense of purpose at work.

Your promotion formula

- Get-Promoted Framework
- Case examples: application of the framework
- Apply the framework to your current situation

1 Get-Promoted Framework

When I reflect back on the various ways I have helped clients to get their next promotion, I realise there was an underlying pattern emerging and a promotion formula that could apply to any situation. It was always a mixture of big picture, long-term strategy and short-term tactics. Although already successful and senior, my clients presented with a feeling of having lost their way, and a sense that they were stuck in a rut or in danger of plateauing at their current role level, while not yet having fulfilled their leadership potential.

We talked about what they felt their potential was, and what they really wanted from their career. We would get into a conversation about what they really enjoyed, where their true talents lay, and how they wanted to reconnect with a sense of joy and purpose from their work. Up until this conversation, the years of relentless day to day toil and growing feelings of dissatisfaction meant a steady decline in vitality and an erosion of real enjoyment from their work. I would ask my client what was their ultimate dream role, to reconnect them with their higher purpose, and then it was easier for me/us to work out the fastest path to get there. So we always started with the end in mind, and then came back to today's reality to plan the next step. The theme was **'Purpose: why do you want the promotion'**.

The feeling of lost potential was accompanied by a feeling of lack of control over how to resolve. I empowered my clients by explaining that waiting around for the organisation to recognise their brilliance was too passive and obviously not a clear path to success – they needed to take back control of their own career destiny and plan their next move. The theme was **'Empowerment: take charge of your career'**.

I explain all this to you now, so that you see that you too need to start with the bigger picture, dream role in mind and take back control of your career destiny. If you know what you want, it is easier to plot out the path of necessary promotions to get you there. It helps you to feel motivated and it helps you to zone in on the immediate next steps.

I also realised that there was too much focus on current role, and not enough on positioning for promotion to future roles. The theme became **'Positioning: position yourself for future success'**. The most earnest and hard-working managers were so busy and overloaded on current role deliverables that they were missing opportunities to grow and expand and spot the next big career move. So although it seems counterintuitive to the hard-working manager, I needed to advise my clients to do less in terms of current role-thinking, and more on future role-thinking. That does not mean the current role deliverables suffer.

you are doing too much of the doing, and not enough of the leading

If anything, as soon as you start thinking more strategically, you realise that you are doing too much of the doing, and not enough of the leading and there are opportunities to get your team or others to step up and support you better.

The pattern was too much focus on performance, but not enough on everything else it would take to successfully position for promotion. In terms of what it takes to get the immediate next promotion – on your path towards your ultimate dream role – I decided that yes there had to be a solid platform of **Performance** track record and results, and perhaps the need to bring forward some new ideas to impress stakeholders. After that there were also four other critical aspects:

1. **Personal impact** – self-confidence on ability to do the next role (without this, unconscious self-sabotage was rife at every twist and turn);

2. **People** – figuring out who makes the promotion decision and influencing them to choose you;

3. **Politics** – engaging with the politics of the organisation; and

4. **Proactivity** – being proactive about asking for what you want.

That last point, 'proactivity', has proved the hardest for some of my clients. It is much easier for a junior person to ask for what they want. Perhaps it is because they have nothing to lose and everything to gain by displaying ambition. However, I have noticed that the more senior the client, the more courage they need to put themselves out there and declare what they really want in the face of more intense politics higher up the corporate food chain. In any case, it is a vital part of figuring out your next move – when to ask and how.

With all that in mind, I synthesised my experiences into the Get-Promoted Framework, and I am very pleased to share it with you now.

Figure 2.1   Your Get-Promoted™ Framework

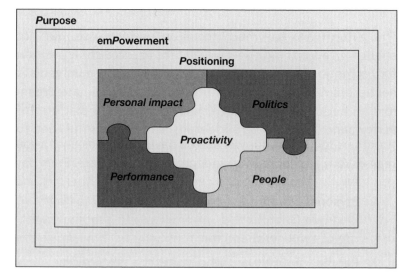

There are three critical parts to the Get-Promoted Framework, which introduce us to 3 of the 7 Ps of promotion success: Purpose, emPowerment and Positioning.

PART 1: PURPOSE – WHY DO YOU WANT THE PROMOTION?

If you can understand and define your higher work purpose, you will have more intrinsic motivation to achieve your promotion goals. With a clear *'why?'* underlying your motivations, you will be more energised and more able to centre your promotion choices on what you want to achieve long term, on what you enjoy, and what drives you. The more motivated you are to achieve your goals, and the more fulfilled you feel, the more energetic and focused you will be – others will notice this renewed vigour and are more likely to promote you. With a long-term vision in mind of what you want to achieve, you will have more clarity and determination when deciding on your next desired promotion.

the more motivated you are to achieve your goals … the more energetic and focused you will be

PART 2: EMPOWERMENT – TAKE CHARGE OF YOUR CAREER

You have to take control and take responsibility for your career and for your promotions. It is a weak non-strategy to simply wait for others to decide your worth. You have more choice than you realise. You can choose what your promotion goals are. Every day you have the choice to make decisions that are either helping you towards achieving your promotion goal, or diverting your attention away from this task. You can't control what happens to you in your work environment, especially the more junior you are, but you can control how you react and respond to it.

PART 3: POSITIONING – POSITION YOURSELF FOR FUTURE SUCCESS

With longer-term goals and dreams in mind, decide on the best next role to help take you there. Once you have decided on your next promotion goal, or a desirable promotion opportunity presents itself to you, then you need to position yourself accordingly for success. You especially need to know that this is about going beyond achieving your current role results to secure what you want:

- **Personal impact:** be confident about your ability to step up
- **People:** figure out who really makes the decision
- **Politics:** stack the odds in your favour
- **Performance:** deliver great results to get attention
- **Proactivity:** put yourself forward for the role.

At this core level, positioning yourself for getting promoted is like figuring out a jigsaw puzzle, where each piece needs to be present, and all need to fit together to form the whole promotion-ready picture. It is important not to neglect any piece of the puzzle. For example, if your Performance is optimal, but you struggle with Politics, then it's more likely you will not get the promotion. And the same can be said for any combination. It will be important to get the calibration right on each P. For example, you can get all the other 4 Ps ready, but if you lack courage on Proactivity then all your efforts will be in vain. Some might say that Politics is more important than Performance, but I wouldn't want to advocate that this is true in all cases.

positioning yourself for getting promoted is like figuring out a jigsaw puzzle

This framework operates as the backbone to the structure of the rest of the book. I go into detail in a dedicated chapter on each of the 7 Ps.

> **The 7 Ps of promotion success**
>
> 1. **P**urpose: Why do you want to be promoted?
> 2. em**P**ower Yourself: Take charge of your career
> 3. **P**ersonal impact: Be confident about your ability to step up
> 4. **P**eople: Figure out who really makes the decision
> 5. **P**olitics: Stack the odds in your favour
> 6. **P**erformance: Deliver great results to get attention
> 7. **P**roactivity: Put yourself forward for the role

We will start with defining your 'Purpose' in the next chapter. But first, let me give you some case examples where these 7 Ps principles were applied.

2 Case examples: application of the framework

I would like to give you an overview of how all the Ps come into play based on some blended examples of client assignments I have worked on. The intention is to focus on two major transitions – from Manager to Director (or replace 'Director' with whatever title constitutes 'senior leader' in your company, e.g. Vice President), and from Director to C-suite (reporting directly to the CEO) – and offer you some potentially relatable examples, in order to demonstrate that you are not the only one who struggles to get what you want. You can also see how the Get-Promoted Framework applies to actual case scenarios. I would like you to start to become familiar with the framework so that it doesn't feel like merely clever management consultancy theory – but is actually a formula applicable to every case example, and that you start to recognise the presence or absence of each of the 7 Ps. The more practised you become at spotting the Ps, the more you can apply the framework to your situation and get-promoted environment.

start to recognise the presence or absence of each of the 7 Ps

EXAMPLE 1 – MANAGER TO DIRECTOR

Mark worked in a financial services consultancy and he hired me because he wanted to get promoted to Director level. His organisation is the kind of competitive pyramid shape where you are expected to move up or move out. He was ambitious to make the promotion transition from Manager to Director to prove that he was 'senior material'. On the one hand, there appeared to be an HR-driven, transparent company promotion process, with a clear set of criteria and dates. On the other hand, what seemed to be common streetwise knowledge in the firm was that, regardless of official criteria, the decision would ultimately come down to whether or not you had a senior sponsor in the room at the time, fighting your corner, when the final decision was being made on promotions. Depending on that sponsor's seniority, and how much influence that person has, their say-so could override everyone else and any formal criteria.

The essence of our how-to-get-Mark-promoted task became as follows:

- Help Mark to significantly increase his client sales revenue in order to meet the minimum threshold to get on to the Director shortlist. All other performance criteria were already met.

- Identify and get the support of the one or two key senior people who would definitely be in the room, and who could potentially vouch for Mark and fight for him versus the many other strong candidates on the promotion shortlist.

Here were the other immediate challenges of the coaching assignment:

- Mark was all talk and no action. We would agree what needed to be done, but he had no follow through on doing it. This was often down to lack of confidence, and sometimes due to a lack of ability to take instructions and creatively run with them.

- Mark was also defensive, and had an unhelpful sense of false entitlement. He would have to commit to making a bigger effort to get the promotion.

- Mark was a people person, very charming but actually not yet good at selling. He found it relatively easy to establish relationships but much harder to close the deal, and also wasted too much time with junior clients on opportunities that never bore fruit.

- Finally, Mark was able to present me with a list of 25 stakeholders involved in the promotion decision, but he had not prioritised who was critically important, and had never met most of them.

How to relate this to the promotion framework

Purpose: Mark wanted to get promoted, because he wanted the outward status and benefits, but he didn't have the real will for it. He wanted it, but had a lot of resistance when it came to doing what it would take to get the promotion. For example, it takes courage to meet senior stakeholders; it takes effort to try to sell larger deals. It was painful for Mark to hear direct feedback on his performance and attitude, and easier to resist than rectify. Mark had not yet engaged with a true sense of purpose on what he wanted from his career and life in terms of intrinsic versus extrinsic motivation. Any obstacles had the power to easily discourage Mark. Rather than see promotion obstacles as learning opportunities, instead each obstacle loomed large as a threat to the existing status quo and sense of complacency. I needed to engage with Mark to find some real personal purpose and motivation for securing the promotion, so that he would put the work in.

emPowerment: Mark needed my help to empower himself to take more charge and take responsibility for his own career destiny and do what it takes to get the promotion. His victim attitude meant he was stuck on blaming others, and already adopting a defensive position should the decision be non-promotion.

Personal impact: Mark's key talent was his confident ability to engage with others and his likeability, so here was something we could really work with.

People: It would be necessary to get Mark to build a relationship fast with the two key people who were linked to his organisation unit and would be in the meeting room at promotion decision time. Given his strength on personal impact, I was not concerned about Mark's abilities in this regard.

Politics: We had a streetwise read on the politics in terms of how the promotion decisions were really made. Mark also solicited advice and opinions from those who made Director the previous year. From this we learned that a colleague had been promoted without the minimum sales revenue criteria but because she had presented an investment pitch for a very creative revenue-generating idea for the firm. Perhaps this was something we could replicate if Mark failed to meet the minimum threshold amount on sales revenue.

Performance: Mark was doing a reasonably good job, but was not taking advantage of opportunities to showcase his results outside his team.

Proactivity: Mark needed to be more proactive in reaching out to senior colleagues. He needed to tell people he wanted the promotion. He needed to put people under pressure to support his advancement, and ask them for help in influencing the key stakeholders.

What happened next?

Mark set up a senior client introduction dinner with one of his key internal promotion stakeholders. This was a great opportunity to build a strong accelerated relationship with his stakeholder – because there would be briefing meetings prior to and post the dinner, which offered Mark an opportunity to impress and bond with his stakeholder.

Mark's other major internal stakeholder was very keen on the diversity and inclusion agenda within his practice, so Mark volunteered to participate in a working group and built a strong relationship with this sponsor on the back of that.

Note the progress on emPowerment, Proactivity, Politics and People.

Within a few months of great tactical positioning for success and stakeholder campaigning, Mark had made it onto the promotion longlist, but was still short on sales revenue so lacked a real wow factor in terms of why he should get the promotion over and above others on the list with higher sales figures. So we focused on showcasing his leadership potential instead. We looked at the Group CEO agenda to try to work out what concerned him, and where the growth opportunities were for the firm. We discovered that the CEO wanted to build a dedicated new advisory practice in the area of Corporate Ethics & Trust. This was a topic area that immediately connected with Mark. He had finally found a connection to a real purpose. Instead of feeling as if he was just constantly building spreadsheets, here was something he felt he would be proud of and could influence, and a subject matter area where he could really shine.

Mark felt that by getting involved in this new practice area, it would also open up a career path on a specialist niche that was a current hot topic but had longevity as well. He could eventually become an industry speaker and guru on the topic. So I encouraged Mark to contact his promotion stakeholders to say that although he was a little short on the sales threshold, if he was promoted he would seek to play an active leadership role in growing the new Corporate Ethics & Trust practice. On his own initiative, he pitched his vision for the new practice area to stakeholders – including how it could be best organised, and a number of creative ideas on how to bring it to market. In the end it was a close call, but with a successful people campaign under way and impressed by his initiative on a topic prioritised within the CEO agenda, Mark was promoted.

Note that all the pieces of the Get-Promoted Framework were in place:

Purpose – finding a personal connection to a real agenda that has career longevity and deep meaning to you.

emPowerment – shifting from blaming others, to making choices and taking back control.

Personal impact – making a positive impression early on, building trust quickly.

People – getting in front of the major stakeholders and building relationships fast.

Politics – not relying on HR rules alone, but understanding that sponsorship in the room was critical.

Performance – a track record, short on sales but overcome with use of creativity and ideas for a new practice.

Proactivity – making it happen, not becoming discouraged, willing to try new angles.

EXAMPLE 2 – DIRECTOR TO C-SUITE

Jenny had done well in her career but had always assumed she would become a CEO one day. Although she had been quickly promoted through the junior ranks, and was now well established as a director of the firm, it seemed to Jenny that her career was stagnating. She realised she simply didn't know the promotion 'rules' of how to move out of director ranks and into C-suite and eventually secure the role of Group CEO. She could have chosen to be happy with her success to date, because she probably could have stayed at her current level for another 10 years, but something in her was dissatisfied about not fully reaching her leadership potential. It also irked her that some of her peers seemed to be on a more upwards career trajectory, while her most recent moves appeared to be more lateral and sideways on level of responsibility, rather than any significant upward moves. Jenny hired me to help her to get promoted.

We agreed that, given her current starting point, she would need a three-step plan to CEO (i.e. it would take three moves to get there), but that an accelerated step one would be to get her promoted to a C-suite functional role as Chief Operating Officer. If she could then move from there into running one of the company's largest business divisions, she would be well placed to become the next Group CEO.

The essence of our how-to-get-Jenny-promoted task became as follows:

- Build a direct relationship with the current Group CEO, and impress him so much that if the vacancy for COO emerged, my client would become the obvious choice.

- Build a groundswell of goodwill towards my client so that other senior players would influence the Group CEO, or at a minimum not object if the Group CEO discussed the possibility of appointing my client to the C-suite.

You may think this is an overly simplistic summary of what needed to be done. But, in truth, if you want to get into the C-suite it is within the gift of the incumbent CEO and essentially you just need to focus on that relationship and those who influence him. At this level, despite what you may be officially told, there is no real company process on promotions. Jobs are not usually advertised, and conversations on succession are held behind closed doors, and – while always rationalised by Group HR afterwards, e.g. that all views were solicited, that succession plans were consulted, that up to three candidates were considered, etc. – it is often based on timing and the whim of the big boss.

Here were the immediate challenges of the assignment:

- My client would not ask the CEO for the role. It emerged that my client had a core confidence issue on moving forward. My client did not feel comfortable articulating her vision for the future of the firm to the incumbent CEO – afraid he might be offended rather than delighted by her initiative.

- My client was happy to lobby for the support of all other stakeholders, anyone and everyone except the CEO (!).

- There were no other immediate challenges in the coaching assignment.

How to relate this to the promotion framework

Purpose: Jenny wanted to eventually become a CEO because she wanted to make a difference. She felt she had a strategic vision for her industry and that her organisation had already become overly bureaucratic, faced threat from new competitors, and was no longer in prime growth mode. Jenny felt she would instil a more commercial edge in her leadership team as CEO, and felt she could encourage a better set of leadership behaviours and values. Her purposefulness drove her to continue to want the promotion, and in the end it was her unhappiness with career stagnation and this intrinsic motivation to make a difference which finally got Jenny out of her comfort zone and into a conversation with the Group CEO on her next move.

emPowerment: Jenny was very nervous about asking the CEO for the role. It actually took one year of personal coaching and support before Jenny would have the courage to do this. If that seems like a long time to you, then you are right, but be careful not to judge too harshly. At this senior level, the stakes are very high, and the fear of rejection is more intense. Also my client had to feel confident that, if she was given the role, she could actually do it!

Personal impact: Jenny had a good energy about her, had built up a good reputation through years of hard work and productivity, and was already very popular within the firm.

People: Jenny had no problem working out where others' views might lie in terms of her promotion prospects and garnering their support. But unfortunately she was deeply intimidated by the idea of speaking so frankly with the Group CEO about her own career ambitions. To her, it felt too brash and she would rather have been talent-spotted by the CEO. But guess what, that hadn't happened to date, so staying passive would not be a smart strategy and I had to convince Jenny on that.

Politics: Jenny had been in the firm long enough to know how to handle people culturally and what would work politically or not in terms of approaching different people – including her own boss, and the chief executives of the major business divisions, and group HR. She was savvy enough to know how to approach her stakeholders, and know what to say to gain their support for her upwards move.

Performance: Jenny had already proved herself over and over again on results, so current role performance was not an issue. However, to get into the C-suite we felt that Jenny needed to write a paper on her vision on the future of the firm so as to be taken as a serious contender for the C-suite.

Proactivity: Jenny had a real problem with proactivity with the one stakeholder that really mattered – the CEO. She struggled with the courage to simply ask him for the COO role.

What happened next?

It took 12 months for me to persuade Jenny to make her pitch to the CEO. During that time she did a good job of getting every other stakeholder onside. Their support for her helped a lot with her confidence levels. Plus she knew she was running out of time, as the current COO had signalled his potential retirement, having been in the role for over four years. Jenny finally made her move. She presented a three-year vision for what she would do as COO and a list of priorities for the first 12 months. The CEO was impressed with her ideas and her track record. Within six months of asking the CEO for the role of COO, the vacancy arose and my client was appointed.

Note that all the pieces of the Get-Promoted Framework were in place:

Purpose – Jenny knew why she was taking up the role of COO as a three-step career game plan to get promoted to CEO where she felt she could make a significant difference and fulfil her leadership potential. She wanted to demonstrate a more collaborative approach to leadership, improve the culture and return the firm to its former prime position in the industry.

emPowerment – Jenny knew that being passive was not working for her, and she empowered herself to take charge of her career destiny. At first Jenny tried to outsource the problem to me, as if by hiring me I would somehow 'fix' the problem. Instead I advised and supported Jenny on what she had to do.

Personal impact – Jenny was a credible executive, an intelligent person and a popular choice.

People – Jenny had launched a successful campaign with the CEO influencers, so that when the CEO sense-checked her candidacy for the COO role, no one objected or was overly surprised to hear that she was a candidate under consideration.

Politics – Jenny had a lot of tacit knowledge on how to deal with people in her organisation. She was aware of who else might be considered for the role, but she did not waste time worrying about the competition or engaging in any low-level politics. Jenny simply focused on what was best for the firm when writing her vision paper on the role of the COO to support the future growth of the company.

Performance – She had a strong track record and some big leadership ideas in her presentation of her vision of the firm.

Proactivity – My client (finally) asked the right person for the promotion.

3 Apply the framework to your current situation

I have provided you with two examples of major promotion transitions – from Manager to Director, and from Director to C-suite – in the hope that something in those examples of classic transitions relates to your situation. At a very minimum,

I want you to get comfortable with applying the Get-Promoted Framework to case examples, and then to your own situation.

what is your 'I-want-to-get-promoted' story?

What is your 'I-want-to-get-promoted' story, and do you feel you can start to identify and recognise the presence or absence of the 7 Ps in your career right now?

Although you have not yet read through the detailed explanation of what I mean by each P, take a pulse check now on where you think you are in relation to each of them. Rate your effectiveness in terms of how you are currently applying each P to your promotion prospects – and where the opportunity areas lie for improvement. If, by chance, this gives you an immediate eureka moment on what you need to be doing tomorrow, even before reading the rest of the book, then great!

THE 7 Ps	RATE YOUR EFFECTIVENESS (HIGH, MEDIUM OR LOW) ON HOW YOU ARE CURRENTLY APPLYING EACH P TO YOUR PROMOTION PROSPECTS:
Purpose: why do you want the promotion?	
emPower yourself: take charge of your career	
Personal impact: be confident about your ability to step up	
Politics: stack the odds in your favour	
People: figure out who really makes the decision	
Performance: deliver great results to get attention	
Proactivity: put yourself forward for the role	

With that rating in mind, let's delve more deeply into each of the 7 Ps over the following seven chapters, and you can become more familiar with how I define them, and how you can grow in your understanding of how each applies to your situation.

3

Purpose: why do you want the promotion?

- Set out a vision for your career
- Promotion is about a path to leadership
- Your key task: develop your career game plan

1 Set out a vision for your career

Have you really thought about why you want a promotion? Rather than take a job simply because it comes with a pay rise, try to step back and think strategically about what you want from your whole career. Sometimes a quick promotion – for example, when it involves moving to a smaller-sized company – might seem like a great get-promoted idea in the short term, but might there be limits placed on your future career prospects? On the other hand, in a smaller set-up, perhaps you have the opportunity to make a bigger impact and feel more fulfilled. Whatever the situation, before focusing on your next role, pause and take a more strategic perspective on your long-term career desires. Think about your overall career vision and how your next role could be set in that context.

take a more strategic perspective on your long-term career desires

- What is your eventual dream role?

- Are you on the path to achieving it?

- Do you have a higher work purpose to fulfil?

- Do you want a job, a career or to fulfil your vocation?

- Are you proud of what you do, and what you want to do next?

- In the future when you look back at your legacy, will your career have been worthy of all the energy you put into it?

This may sound dramatic at first – after all, you only read this book to get a promotion, not to think about your legacy! Perhaps it does seem a bit over the top if right now you are running a call centre and concerned primarily with a promotion for the

think more strategically about what you want your work legacy to be

pay rise that will help pay the mortgage. But I urge you to take a moment to step back now, and try to think more strategically about what you want your work legacy to be – before you take the next promotion step in your career path. If you can work out what you want your work legacy to be, you will be able to dig deeper to pursue your immediate goals and therefore are more likely to achieve them. Why shouldn't you take your career seriously? You spend a lot of time at work. It would be good to feel that you are nurturing your soul, and working towards ultimate career fulfilment, as well as paying your living expenses.

HAVE A LONG-TERM MINDSET

A long-term mindset will help you to find the energy and drive to get promoted in the short term, because you will be able to put any challenges or obstacles into perspective with regard to the greater end goal. The petty politics of today's meetings are less likely to upset you if you know that you are on the path to greater things. By starting with the ultimate end in mind, you can free yourself up to be as ambitious as you like.

by starting with the ultimate end in mind, you can free yourself up to be as ambitious as you like

---

Examples of higher work purpose

'To fulfil my leadership potential.'

'To unleash the potential of others.'

'To make a difference.'

▶

'To influence.'

'To change the world.'

'To transform the quality of customer service.'

'To connect the world.'

'To improve the role of business in society.'

Figure 3.1 Discover your higher work purpose

What are your passions and interests?
What brings you joy?
When do you feel most fulfilled at work?
Who inspires you?
What do you want to achieve with your life?

Write your Personal Mission Statement – and reset your promotion priorities accordingly.

If you can make the connection between your personal mission and the mission of the organisation, then you have struck personal and career gold! The more aligned you are with the goals of the organisation, the more likely you are to be happier, highly engaged and motivated, and the more likely the organisation is going to want to keep you around and keep promoting you.

Career Gold = Personal Enjoyment + Engagement + Motivation = Increased Work Success = Organisation and Personal Interests Aligned = Promotion!

BE AUTHENTIC

If you think more deeply about what impact you want to have through your life's work, then you will have a better perspective on what role you want to do next and why. The more you can bring your soul to work, the more you will be at ease with your work identity, and the more likely you are to be successful at work. Organisations are becoming flatter and more democratic, so fear is out, and authentic leadership is in. Young people are demanding more

fear is out ... authentic leadership is in

sincerity from their leaders, so senior organisation promotions are being based much more on character. Living your values is a prerequisite as much as, if not more than, having a strategic brain. Generation Y want to feel that they are working towards meaningful goals, with leaders who are true role models. The modern would-be leader has got to feel authentic to his followership, and since it is quite hard to fake authenticity, it would be much easier for you to get clear on your core values and line up your career plans accordingly.

The desire for authenticity is good news for everyone, because what it means is you no longer have to try to be some cookie-cutter version of what the nineties said a manager or leader should be. You simply need to be yourself, and to build on your personal strengths and attributes, and experiences. You need to be able to lead, of course, but your ability to inspire and motivate others to follow will be coming from your personal energy rather than just a reliance on command and control structure.

DEVELOP YOUR CAREER GAME PLAN

With a long-term mindset, and an authentic approach to what really matters to you, consider your career game plan. Think about where you are now, and what would be the next role to set you on the path towards the end goal. For example, I was working with a Managing Director whose dream was to become Group CEO. When I asked her what prior role it would take to get promoted to Group CEO, she said it would have to be an operational role such as being the President of one of their biggest market operating units. The best route to becoming President of a sizeable operating unit is to secure a role as the Finance Director of that operating unit, and then COO of that operating unit. So her game plan became: get promoted to Finance Director of Americas, get promoted to President of Americas, get promoted to Group CEO. Shifting from no plan to an actual game plan can be very liberating. It focuses the mind and behaviour in the current role to think about what she needs to do now, to be worthy of each of the next roles.

Table 3.1 Your career game plan

CAREER VISION EXAMPLE: 'TO BECOME GROUP CEO BY 2025'		
GAME PLAN	ROLE	BY WHEN
Ultimate Desired Role:	Group CEO	Within 10 years
Bridging Role:	President of Major Region	Within 5 years
Next Role:	Chief Operating Officer	Within 3 years
Desired Promotion:	Finance Director	Within 12 months
Current Role:	Senior Manager, Finance	

The strategy of thinking big is more tactical than you might think. Your superiors want to promote someone who has leadership ambition. After all, from their point of view, every promotion point is an investment in you as a potential leader of the firm. By being ambitious – and by communicating your ambition – and having a game plan, others will be impressed by you. You need to believe in yourself. After all, why would others put their faith in you as an investment bet for the future, if you don't have faith in yourself? With your game plan in mind, and your sights set on the next role promotion, let's delve further into how you position yourself for promotion success.

Advice from the top

Professionals should have a purpose – particularly at executive level. Companies have a purpose. Why not people? If you are looking for someone who's inspirational at a senior level ... someone who doesn't have a purpose isn't going to be inspirational. If I can paint a picture of where I want us to go, and you follow me up the hill, that's far more successful than me pushing you up the hill.

ARIEL ECKSTEIN, MANAGING DIRECTOR, LINKEDIN

Be purposeful about how you want to conduct your life and what you want your career to be, but don't be too formulaic. I'm quite a spontaneous person and reflecting back on my career, I think I may have progressed further and more quickly, if I had been a little bit more purposeful with my career. Early on I had the wrong impression that people would just notice what a good job I was doing and promote me.

In our organisation, there's a lot of emphasis placed on people getting different experience in their careers. You know, emerging market experience as well as western market experience. Different functional experience is essential, rather than going from, for example, just sales roles to CEO.

Be very good at what you do. Be confident, don't be arrogant. It's about keeping everything balanced. It's about people knowing that you are keen for your career to move on and that you are ambitious, but you need to recognise that you need to be contributing successfully to the business. Someone who keeps that balance right, between having an eye on how their career is progressing,

▶

but understanding that it's predicated by doing a good job, developing people and their team and contributing to the business is well positioned for promotion to the top.

JANE GRIFFITHS, GROUP CHAIRMAN,
JANSSEN PHARMACEUTICAL

Know yourself and know what your purpose is. Reflect on the leadership that you've already done, and really think about what drives you and excites you and what you really want to do. That's the platform for your next role. If you know yourself, and you've given a lot of prior thought to thinking through your purpose, you will already have an answer when people ask you what you want at the critical moment. This means that when you need to think and act fast, when you might otherwise be flustered, the tactical career decisions come automatically.

Think about what you are not willing to compromise on, and think about whether you are in the right organisation. In most UK-based organisations in 2015, unless there are serious institutional problems, being yourself, and your identity – male, female, ethnic minority, LGBT or disabled – can be a vehicle and an added resource for personal impact. Even in a corporate male-dominated environment, it can set you apart, it gives you differentiation. Think about if there is a project you can initiate. Ask yourself what is your identity, and can you use it to set yourself apart and add value where others can't.

STEPHEN FROST, VISITING FELLOW AT HARVARD
UNIVERSITY & HEAD OF DIVERSITY
AND INCLUSION, KPMG

2 Promotion is about a path to leadership

Everyone wants to get promoted, and this eventually means getting on the path to leadership. Take a moment to let that really sink in. If you want to continue to get promotions then you will need to have the courage and competency to eventually lead people and teams. The more senior you become, the more likely you are to be setting the vision, and leading a team of hundreds or maybe thousands of people. That is a heady position of responsibility and influence. Is this what you want? Early on in your career, technical expertise will be what wins you promotions, but as you progress, you will need to be able to switch from reliance on your technical and functional knowledge to being able to manage and lead others. I am not trying to put you off. I am actually trying to get you ahead of the game. I am pointing out to you that, by being ambitious for promotions, you are deciding that in the future you want to be a leader, and that you will be dropping your emphasis on functional and technical expertise and improving your ability to get the best out of others. If that is fine with you, then it is never too soon to think about what kind of leader you want to be, and to really invest in yourself now to improve on how you manage and lead other people.

- Do you want to be a leader?
- What kind of leader do you want to be?

what kind of leader do you want to be?

- Are you up for making the switch from functional expertise to leadership expertise?
- Do you possess the modern leadership skills necessary to get promoted in today's environment?

INVEST NOW IN YOUR PEOPLE MANAGEMENT SKILLS

I am emphasising the point that promotions are about a path to leadership because, for some strange reason, this is not always clearly spelled out by the organisation. There is so much emphasis on technical skill at the junior level that very often, just a few roles later, people 'find themselves' managing others without much training at all on how to be a good people manager. As early on as possible and ahead of being in the situation of managing large numbers of people, if you can encourage company investment in you on people management skills, or privately invest your own funds in yourself on courses outside the company, then you can stand out from your peers and get a great reputation as a people person. This kind of differentiation will be crucial for future promotion prospects.

START BEHAVING LIKE A LEADER

You don't need to have been promoted to a leadership position yet to start behaving like a leader. You can be a leader among your peers. You can shine out as having leadership potential. Redefine your current job in order to make more strategic contributions. Get your team working harder for you. Free up time and space to allow for new ideas. Perhaps you have a big idea on a new company growth area (visionary leadership skills), perhaps **free up time and space to allow for new ideas** you notice that the organisation is missing the big picture on new disruptive technologies (strategic leadership skills), or perhaps you are simply great at motivating and managing people (people leadership skills).

Start behaving like a leader

Be visionary: Talk about the future and possibilities.

Be strategic: See the bigger picture, focus on long-term goals.

Be authentic: Bring your real self to work.

Inspire others: Motivate and enthuse others.

Get the best out of those around you: Encourage others to speak their mind. Praise people when they do a good job.

Run operations effectively: Meet your targets.

Push boundaries – challenge constructively: At meetings, be alert and listen, and contribute only when it is useful to others. In other words, don't speak for the sake of talking. Less is more.

Bring energy to meetings – be an optimist: When you raise an issue or a problem, also bring options on how to solve.

3 Your key task: develop your career game plan

Depending on what rank you are now, give yourself 3–5 moves only. Reduce the amount of time in each role, in order to accelerate to the next role. For example, if the norm in your company is to spend 3–5 years in each role, then think about what it would take to do the role for 2–3 years.

YOUR CAREER VISION: 'TO BECOME…'		
GAME PLAN	ROLE	BY WHEN
Ultimate Desired Role:		
Bridging Role:		
Next Role:		
Desired Promotion:		
Current Role:		

Advice from the top

When you're considering your next leadership role, you should have a clear view of what the role after that is that you want, and how this next promotion helps you achieve the one after that. This is a critical thing to think about when you are a leader. There comes a point where you need to be a bit more articulate about what it is that you want to do. You can be a generic leader and let your stakeholders know that you are ready for the next challenge, but there also comes a time when you need to be a bit more focused and specific about what you want.

VIMI GREWAL-CARR, MANAGING PARTNER
FOR INNOVATION AND DELIVERY MODELS,
DELOITTE CONSULTING

Getting promoted is about good leadership, fairness, authenticity, respect and honesty – these are all things about you as a person rather than your ability to perform your specific role, which is obviously important too. Being somebody that people want to work with, and being respected is extremely important. Very often the reason that someone doesn't get a promotion can come down to people not wanting to work with them. On top of this, you need to focus on breadth and demonstrating the ability to operate at the next level. It's really important to use your curiosity to broaden your knowledge and understanding beyond your core competency. If you spend a long time in a narrow functional job, there will come a time when you want to be promoted to the next level and you're going to be asked to make judgements about things that you aren't familiar with.

MAI FYFIELD, CHIEF STRATEGY OFFICER, SKY

For me there are three important points. Firstly, you need to be able to be yourself, and that means that you have your own unique point of view. In my experience, senior people do not like people who say yes to everything. You need to have your own view, and your own ideas, and not be afraid to voice them. Secondly, you need to be able to say 'no'. This may be unique to our type of organisation, but you need to be able to say no, and ask for help – be that resources or otherwise – when needed. And finally, you need to have a network of people who know you and who support you, because they recognise your leadership potential and they are happy to work with you. These three points are on top of the obvious key requirement – which for me is 'performance'. You need to perform at the top, so in order to get to the top, you need to perform.

PETER SKODNY, COUNTRY MANAGING
DIRECTOR, ACCENTURE

Today's modern leader needs to be accessible, authentic, and completely consistent with their behaviours.

IAN POWELL, CHAIRMAN AND
SENIOR PARTNER AT PWC

Always try to have your next two steps in mind. Always deliver and execute with excellence, and it's a cliché, but surround yourself with good people. When building your team as a leader you should source talent internally and externally and get experts in. Leading a talented team to success will help get you noticed and having the right story, and the ability to tell it in the right way will bring opportunities.

COLUM HONAN, DIRECTOR OF OPERATIONS,
MEDICAL DEVICE COMPANY

4

emPowerment: take charge of your career

- Take back control
- Create, don't wait
- Your key task: make a list of empowering strategies

1 Take back control

Early on in your career, you may have been strictly guided by company processes and HR policies. You may have had formal or informal mentors who cared about your success and nurtured your talent as a junior. However, as you climb the corporate ranks, you can't always rely on others to appreciate you and validate you. At senior levels, everyone is busy, busy, busy. It's time for you to grow up and take charge of your own career destiny. It isn't the job of others to prop you up and constantly reassure you that you are worthy and doing a good job. If you want to reach and succeed at more senior levels, you need to take back control and empower yourself.

it's time for you to grow up and take charge of your own career destiny

In all corporate environments you need to have a thick skin – i.e. you need to be able to stand up for yourself; not take things personally; defend yourself in meetings; stand up for what you believe in; fight your corner on budget and resources; and know what you are capable of delivering for the organisation. The same goes for promotion. You need to believe in yourself and go for it. The pyramid shape of the organisation – with fewer roles on the top than on the bottom – means that competition for roles increases and the question becomes *'what do you have to offer – above your peers – that means we should invest in you?'* You need to empower yourself with the answer to that question so that your promotion prospects remain strong. But first, fire up your inner resolve and decide now to take charge of your own career. It is never too early to start doing this.

you need to believe in yourself and go for it

Advice from the top

Early in their career, people very often externalise why they have had success. They attribute success to a good boss they had, or simply luck. You've got to recognise at some point that you are responsible for your success, and more importantly, that you are in control of it, and your career.

GARETH MCWILLIAMS, GENERAL MANAGER
OPERATIONS, BT BUSINESS/SME

FIRE UP YOUR INNER RESOLVE

Your inner resolve is about simply deciding you are good enough for promotion and you are going to go for it. Look around you – no rows and rows of rocket scientists surrounding your cubicle, I am guessing. I am sure you are just as good, if not even better than your peers. At the very least, you have potential and are willing to learn. Look at the folks above you. Yes, some are impressive for sure, but not all. The more exposure you have to senior people the more you see their flaws. We often, wrongly, put senior leaders on a pedestal, bestowing virtues upon them that are not at all deserved. Take them off the pedestal and see more clearly what they are good at, and what they are not good at. Realise that they have strengths and weaknesses just like you. Resolve to give this promotion your best shot, that you compare well with others and perhaps even better than most. Never forget: *'If that guy can do it, so can I.'*

Once you have fixed your inner resolve, then your intention is more stable and focused. By simply deciding that you definitely want the promotion, you increase the likelihood that you are going to get it. By deciding you want it, you are more likely to take the necessary steps to get it. This energy also transmits consciously (through your actions) and unconsciously (through your energy) to others. The decision-makers will see it and feel it from you, and will be more likely to be impressed by your keenness to get the role.

By taking charge, you will stop being passive and also avoid acting like a victim. Waiting for the call-up that never happens is very disappointing and can lead to bitterness and regret later on. Blaming others and acting like a victim is also detrimental to your well-being. You have more control over your promotion prospects than you realise.

2 Create, don't wait

Rather than wait for the annual promotion round, or wait for the nod from the higher-ups, or wait for some kind of reassuring signal – my advice is don't wait for anything. Create, don't wait. Create an opportunity to propel your career forward. Sometimes by being creative you can get a promotion faster, **my advice is don't wait for anything** and even skip a level. By taking action, you are taking charge and step by step you are creating the desired outcome.

Examples of empowering strategies

- Just ask
- Impress your boss
- Craft a new role
- Unlock your network
- Join a new company
- Give yourself a promotion
- Offer to take an overseas assignment
- Make your existing role more strategic

JUST ASK

Have you ever actually asked for a promotion? Sometimes, you simply have to ask the right person in the right way, at the right time, and you can immediately fast track your chances for promotion. Don't believe me? It has happened. I worked with a Managing Director who wanted a promotion to a Chief Strategy Officer role, but had never asked for it. I persuaded him to book half an hour with the Group CEO during lunchtime at the next company leadership development event, and present his vision for the future of the firm and his corresponding pitch for promotion. This was tactical timing, because I knew the event would be focused on building the morale of leaders, and therefore the CEO would be in the right mindset and open to encouraging ideas from up-and-coming leaders. My client went to the meeting, armed with a thoughtful presentation, and he made a strong impression. The meeting was a runaway success. It took a further six months for the role vacancy to come up, but when it did, the Group CEO knew exactly who he wanted in post and my client got the call-up. Without putting himself forward for the role, he would never have even been considered.

you can immediately fast track your chances for promotion

If you get an immediate negative response, then ask the decision-maker for advice on how to get the promotion. Get him to tell you what it would take to get promoted, and what advice he can offer you. You need to get him to emotionally commit to your journey. The more the decision-maker feels as if he is responsible for guiding you, the more likely he will feel under pressure to support your promotion.

get him to emotionally commit to your journey

IMPRESS YOUR BOSS

On the face of it, this should be self-evident. Please your boss and she will promote you. However, it is a bit tricky when the only promotion opportunity available would be to take your boss's role. So, yes, please your boss, but work out when, if ever, she intends to leave her post, whether she would want you as her successor, or whether you would be better off to solicit her support on taking a promotion role elsewhere in the company. The problem is that **you need to read between the lines**. Does your boss say she wants you as successor, but she doesn't intend to leave her role for at least another five years? Do you really want to hang around for that long, on such a promise? Does your boss say you are not good enough to do her role, when in reality she may feel threatened that you are more than capable of filling her shoes? How do you resolve the dilemma? Put simply, if pleasing your boss did not get you any closer to promotion within the past two to three years, and if there is no clear promotion in sight within the next six months, then it's time to find a new boss!

Table 4.1 How to impress your boss

10 TOP TIPS – HOW TO IMPRESS YOUR BOSS
1. Offer to take some of her workload
2. Bring the solution as well as the problem
3. Be an optimist
4. Don't embarrass your boss by challenging her in front of others at meetings – you can challenge upwards, but always be constructive
5. Be consistent – no surprises
6. Be drama-free
7. Do what you say you're going to do
8. Be loyal – don't gossip about your boss
9. Be a team player
10. Take the initiative

Case example
Get your boss to commit to you

MUIREANN – RISK MANAGER TO VP OF RISK

Early in her career, Muireann joined a FTSE100 financial services company and developed her expertise in risk analysis. After a couple of years as an individual contributor in a regional office, Muireann heard on the grapevine that a former boss was building a team in the company's London office – the company headquarters. Muireann applied for the Risk Manager role.

With the right track record, and the right connection, Muireann was promoted into the new role. Muireann settled into her new role believing that she now had a good understanding of how promotion works in the company and that this was the first of many promotions that she would be given. Muireann would work hard, jobs would come up, Muireann would apply for them and compete with other candidates and then, hopefully, she would get promotion. Or so she thought.

After three years, it became evident to her that this strategy wasn't working. There was no clear path for her to progress further upwards. She prepared a speech for her boss. One Friday afternoon, Muireann spotted her boss alone in his office and approached him. Muireann started her speech: 'I think I'm valuable to the firm, but I don't think the firm values me.' Muireann could see that her boss was taken by surprise, but she persisted. She described the type of role that she wanted, and told him the title she wanted – a Vice President (VP) role. That Friday afternoon, Muireann and her boss mapped

▶

out how Muireann could achieve the promotion she wanted. Muireann implemented the strategy and took on more responsibility, raised her profile, and eight months later was promoted to VP.

Muireann didn't just ask for the role, she didn't just impress her boss; she also successfully put pressure on her boss to emotionally commit to taking action.

CRAFT A NEW ROLE

In my experience, the easiest way to get a new promotion is to invent a new role. Have you tried this? Lots of companies don't have a Chief Operating Officer (COO) role on the management team, and it is the kind of role that can be crafted to suit your own strengths. It is a fantastic 'catch all' opportunity to pitch to alleviate some of the pressures your boss is under. Think about what responsibilities you could put under the COO role that would make your boss's life easier. A pitch that is a win for your boss is more likely to succeed.

the easiest way to get a new promotion is to invent a new role

I worked with a director who felt aggrieved, and disillusioned by lack of recognition, and had been previously passed over a year before for a 'promised' promotion. I advised him to propose a new role of COO on the management team, describe his vision for it, list the accountabilities that would fall under the role and – if appropriate – subtly play on his boss's guilt for previously passing him over. It took one well-prepared conversation with his boss for this appointment to be made – much to the shock and surprise of his peers. Just by asking the right person in the right way, at the right time, my client secured a great position and platform for future success.

Another interesting angle on how to craft a role is to propose for 'Chief of Staff'. It sounds good, doesn't it, but what is it? No one really knows, and that is why it could be a great idea and opportunity for promotion. You know the pressures your boss is under, and what priority areas are difficult for him to cover. So propose that you become his Chief of Staff and offer to take his problem areas within the scope of your role, as well as people issues and new projects. Your boss may feel relieved, and might just buy it! At a minimum, he will appreciate your empathy, initiative and ambition. Don't be inhibited by the idea of creating a brand new role. If your boss wants it to happen, he will figure it out with his boss and HR.

A more junior version of this could be to propose the new role of 'Program Manager', and bring in certain responsibilities under this new role, such as innovation or new projects.

UNLOCK YOUR NETWORK

By unlocking your internal and external network, you may discover that someone has a vacancy on their team. Make a list of who you know, in positions above you, both inside and outside your company. Pay particular attention to those you worked with and were friendly with in your company, and who have since moved onwards and upwards elsewhere. Go through the list and create a top ten based on criteria of how senior they are and how much they liked or

by unlocking your internal and external network, you may discover that someone has a vacancy on their team

rated you – even if you feel you only made a fleeting positive impression years ago. Now track them all down via online social platforms or whatever it takes, and ask if you could buy them lunch or a coffee and catch up. You might be pleasantly surprised to discover that most people are open to this kind of networking. For those who have no interest, then you know they wouldn't have been helpful in finding you a promotion. For those who are happy to meet you, you can start off with mutual updates and then you can explain that you are keen to move on up in your career and do they have any advice, or do they know of any opportunities that might exist.

Case example

SHAY AND HIS VIEW ON HOW SENIOR PROMOTIONS REALLY WORK

One of the challenges in organisations today is how to be more transparent at senior levels about how promotions are made. Are we really building the right diverse teams, and doing the right things, given that a lot of what I can see actually does come down to people recruiting from their personal networks?

As an example, for one of his previous promotions a few years ago, Shay joined the senior leadership team in a financial advisory firm as an external recruit. The CEO of the company was also new to the company and was building a new team to lead the business. The CEO hired 10 new senior executives for 10 leadership roles. Of those 10, seven new hires had previously worked with the CEO in some capacity and were part of his network. Shay was one of three who had not had a previous relationship with the CEO. But Shay had a connection with the company's Chief Financial Officer who had a relationship with the new CEO.

To further emphasise the point, the CEO had been recruited for his role by the outgoing CEO, with whom he had a long-standing business relationship. In Shay's experience people hire people they know, people they like, and above all people they know they can trust to do a good job and deliver. On top of that, good leaders have a succession plan in place from early in their role, and they more often than not turn to their network for their successor.

Shay's advice to anyone on how to make this informal system work for you is to constantly expand and nurture your relationships inside and outside the company.

JOIN A NEW COMPANY

You could get a promotion by switching company. However, if you want a step-up promotion by switching companies, it often comes with a step-down on company brand. Think about when it is most useful for your career to trade down on company brand for a level-up promotion. If you do it too early, you might find it harder to navigate any route back into a better company brand other than by taking a lateral move or possibly a demotion.

you could get a promotion by switching company

Also it may be easier to get a promotion by joining a new company rather than by getting promoted internally, but if you haven't really earned it what happens if you get found out within a year and then lose that job? Do you plan to company-hop your way through your career? When I look at a curriculum vitae (CV) I can spot the pattern of the person who has been promoted to senior levels through the strategy of joining big brand companies and then switching industries or companies every two or three years. To be honest, I am concerned about the substance of such people – why do they have to deploy this strategy? Are they actually pushed to go, after not meeting expectations? But, frankly, yes, it does work as a promotion strategy. Not all employers notice or share my concern about people with this kind of CV. Headhunters blind the prospective employers with talk of the great brands they have come from, and why the employer should hire them.

Joining a new company will get you out of your comfort zone, and often comes with an attractive sign-on bonus or better salary. However, there is a risk that it may not work out. Many people perform well in their existing company by virtue of the goodwill that they have built up over a number of years. Without this reservoir of goodwill in a new place, it may be difficult to be as successful. That said, if you feel that your current company is never going to fully recognise your efforts, then you probably have nothing to lose by taking your skills elsewhere.

joining a new company will get you out of your comfort zone

GIVE YOURSELF A PROMOTION

Why wait for others to decide? You could decide – as a visualisation experiment! – that you are already promoted; i.e. decide that you are already promoted to the next level, and see whether this would help you change your attitude and work approach, and increase the likelihood that others can now envisage you at the next level of leadership.

It might sound a bit silly at first, even delusional – but actually, as long as you know that this is just an exercise, it can be an effective empowering strategy in terms of stepping up your performance and behaviour if you start to act as you would if you were operating at the next level up. Would you feel more confident? Would you make better decisions?

Look around you – how does your boss and the other people at the next level up behave? Suddenly, by promoting yourself, you might give yourself permission to have opinions on topics and ideas that previously you felt un-entitled to comment on, given your junior position. You could power forward on having the buzz and freedom from the promotion you want, just by liberating yourself to be that more senior person. In the 'dress for success' genre of books and advice, it is always recommended that if you want a promotion, you should dress as if you already have it. In today's modern corporate environment, dress codes are **decide that you are already promoted to the next level** no longer as clear-cut as that (nowadays the receptionists and personal assistants are often the best dressed!), but if the tip applies to your situation, then why not go for it? Smart-casual could become smarter-casual. In very traditional 'suited up' companies, like consulting or law firms or banking, a smart 'next level up' dresser will be noticed and it could even provide a halo effect in that people will unconsciously assume you are capable of operating at the next level up. You would be surprised what influences some people, and if you are sending out a change of image, different from/better than your peers, the senior people might notice you more.

OFFER TO TAKE AN OVERSEAS ASSIGNMENT

There are usually fantastic promotion opportunities in far-flung regions abroad – at smaller satellite offices or in high-growth emerging markets. At a large global conglomerate, there was a vacancy for a role in the Caribbean. The level was Finance Manager. However, at the time, it was difficult to find suitable candidates who would relocate to this particular part of the world for three years. A young ambitious person read these signs, and decided to put himself forward for the relocation on condition that it came with a promotion to Finance Director. At first, it was refused, but with the right level of insistence and a redefinition of what was expected from the role, he negotiated the promotion to Director level, and subsequently fast-tracked his way to a Director promotion that would otherwise have taken at least three more years to achieve in the United Kingdom. When you are young, and not tied to a particular location, then these are the kinds of risks and moves you should consider for getting ahead as fast as possible.

Experience overseas, and especially in emerging markets, is always going to be a plus in your career. It shows you have independence, courage, and an interest in the wider world. Later on in your career, it will stand out as a clever investment of your time, especially if you work in a global company. Once you have made Director, it becomes easier to get your next senior role, and so on. This guy I mentioned had a career game plan: make Director fast, get international experience under his belt, then work out how to switch from functional expertise to General Management. As it happens, the fastest way to General Manager was to take another ex-patriated role. Ex-pat life may not be for you, but – if you are open – it can offer you a pathway to faster promotions, and very good monetary rewards as well as an amazing life experience.

ex-pat life can offer you a pathway to faster promotions, and very good monetary rewards as well as an amazing life experience

MAKE YOUR EXISTING ROLE MORE STRATEGIC

Perhaps you find yourself at the top of your function in a good title/position, but not really empowered and want to step up to a more strategic role and/or have a seat at the executive management table. In these cases, you can pitch a more strategic definition of your role – accompanied by a promotion. For example, I worked with a Group HR Director to craft a new role of Chief People Officer. I worked with a 'stuck' Marketing Director to craft a new role of Chief Marketing Officer. In both those cases, by outlining a more strategic job description and pitching for it demonstrated to their bosses that they had more to offer and both successfully secured a pay rise and new title, and felt more empowered in their role. It took three months in one case, and a year in the other, because naturally you need to demonstrate real change in their role, as well as making a pretty presentation. However, this approach works. It re-invigorated their career, and was the catalyst for a step change. It also works as a neat way to get your title sorted out, prior to moving outside to a new company. The new company is obliged to offer you the same title role as the one you left, so if you can get the promotion in your existing company before you leave for a new one, that can be a good plan because it may be harder initially to prove yourself in a new company when you don't have a track record and don't yet understand how the power and politics work there.

3 Your key task: make a list of empowering strategies

Apply any insights to your current situation. By taking action, you are empowering yourself to get ahead and get promoted. Write down a list of actions you could take.

EMPOWERING STRATEGIES	ACTION LIST
When am I going to ask my boss for promotion?	
What more can I do to impress my boss?	
What role 'vacancy' could I fill on my boss's management team, accompanied by a new title and promotion?	
What actions can I take to unlock my network and work on building more relationships to create new possibilities?	
Is it time to leave and join a new company?	
Shall I imagine I already have the promotion and check how that impacts my behaviour and contribution?	
How can I find out about role opportunities overseas?	
What is a more strategic title and job description for my current role? Could I put 'Senior' or 'Chief of' in front of my existing title and re-platform the role as a new promotion opportunity?	

5

Personal impact: be confident about your ability to step up

- Appreciate your experience
- Tame your inner critic
- Your key task: develop your value proposition for promotion

1 Appreciate your experience

A promotion is about a step-up role, and naturally because you haven't done the role before, you may feel anxious about whether you could really do it – especially if it involves a significant transition such as managing people or managing a business unit for the first time. The way to gain self-confidence is to appreciate the experience you would bring to the next role. Look back on your whole career history and experience to date to understand the unique experience you have, the major transitions you have already made, your strengths and special talents, and the consequent value you would bring to the new role. Although you may not have done the exact role before, perhaps you have experience and strengths in similar aspects of the role that you can draw on. By evaluating what you have to offer, you can build your core confidence and personal power. You will be more self-assured, and more confident. Once you feel more confident about the evidence that backs up your worthiness for the promotion, others will feel more confident about promoting you.

by evaluating what you have to offer, you can build your core confidence and personal power

---

Your unique value proposition

- Proven track record
- Already operating at next level up
- Key strengths
- Spike (i.e. unique talent)
- Differentiation

PROVEN TRACK RECORD

Look back at your years of experience and synthesise what you have achieved to date. For example, you may have progressed from graduate hire to leading a small team. You may have made the shift from functional expert to General Manager. You may have broader market and international experience.

synthesise what you have achieved to date

Whatever strides you have made, you should gain confidence in the conclusion that to reach this current level you must have got most of it right most of the time. On the basis that you have succeeded this far, then there is no reason to stop achieving now.

Consider the experience you have gained, in terms of any key transitions you have made:

- on people management
- on functional expertise
- on geography
- on new markets experience.

Table 5.1 Your key transitions

WHAT KEY TRANSITIONS HAVE YOU ALREADY MADE?	
FROM...	TO...
Individual contributor/team member...	Managing others
Functional specialist...	General manager
Single geography experience...	International experience
Mature markets experience...	Emerging markets experience

ALREADY OPERATING ON THE NEXT LEVEL UP

If you have already started operating at the next level up, then you can be confident of your ability to move formally into the role. Where possible, offer to take on **offer to take on extra responsibilities prior to formal promotion** extra responsibilities prior to formal promotion. In some companies you need to be already operating at the next level up for at least six months before they promote you. In other words, the promotion follows the evidence of action. So ask your boss for more responsibility within this role. Not only will this please your boss, but as you acquire the experience in a new level of responsibility, you will build your confidence for the next role.

Try to also get exposure to the next level up. Ask if you can accompany your boss to more senior meetings, as his right-hand person/note-taker. By attending these sessions, you will learn from observing how senior leaders behave. It will give you confidence to know that you could participate at that level. I remember the first time I attended a Board Meeting. I was a junior management consultant accompanying my Senior Manager and Client Partner. The client was a major retailer and the whole experience was a real eye opener as I realised that the Board members were simply all trying to please the boss and didn't have the courage to challenge him or bring fresh ideas to the table. I realised then that leaders should never be put on a pedestal. It also gave me confidence that as I continued with my career, then perhaps I could operate – and perhaps even do a better job – at that level, if I always maintained my integrity and spoke up against the groupthink.

KEY STRENGTHS

We all have natural areas of strength. What are you good at? Can you identify your key strengths and link them to the criteria for promotion? Think about what it is that you have to offer, areas of strength that are uniquely yours. At manager level, candidate choices for promotion are typically equally technically competent. So usually the strength areas are about something more than technical expertise. It is more likely to be about your work ethic or your negotiation skills, or your reliability to complete tasks on time, on budget. Think about your behavioural strengths, more so than your technical expertise.

think about what it is that you have to offer, areas of strength that are uniquely yours

Table 5.2 Your key strengths

HOW TO IDENTIFY YOUR STRENGTHS
Think about which areas of your work get most praise. Is it about your subject matter expertise, or your skills with difficult stakeholders, or your comfort with ambiguity, or what is it that others have noticed about you?
Check for patterns of strengths in your performance appraisals.
Ask your boss and colleagues formally and/or informally what s/he thinks your strengths and special talents are.
Go online and search under 'strengths audit tools' to find books and questionnaires that you fill out and receive a feedback report in return. These are usually highly accurate.
Discuss with an executive coach, who can either make their own observations or run an independent feedback exercise with your colleagues on your behalf, or will use various psychometric tools at their disposal. A coach is trained to reveal to you important core insights that others are not professionally qualified to do.

SPIKE (i.e. UNIQUE TALENT)

Everyone has strengths, and even better than strengths are what I call a spike. A strength is an area of above average talent. A spike is a significant strength area where you are exceptionally talented. For example, you may have a natural strength as a people person and team player and your spike could be *'your ability to build senior client relationships very quickly'*. A client of mine is excellent at building senior relationships very quickly. He quickly builds credibility with senior clients and can introduce his boss to the C-suite within months of serving at a new customer site.

It is important to grasp what you are good at and what you are significantly good at, in order to be more self-aware and build confidence around your work identity and what you can offer at a more promoted level. Some might say that it is better to focus more effort on enabling your spike to define you, rather than necessarily flattening out your areas for development. Of course, there is also virtue in being an all-rounder, but that in itself might be your identifiable spike – e.g. *'adaptable, can be trusted in any situation, a competent and safe pair of hands'*.

the spike is your black belt – it's simply what you are hard wired to be good at

The spike is your black belt. It's simply what you are hard wired to be good at.

Table 5.3 Your spike

HOW TO IDENTIFY YOUR SPIKE
When considering all your strengths, did one jump out as being way above average? Do others consistently say the same thing about you, e.g. 'You know what you are *really* good at is…'
Or perhaps you already have your own insight on what you are really good at. Best to sense-check with others to ensure it matches perceptions!

DIFFERENTIATION

Differentiation is about how you stand out from the pack. In a sea of equally competent candidate choices, how do you stand out from your peers? Do you have something that gives you an edge over others? If not, think strategically about how you could gain that between now and promotion decision.

how do you stand out from your peers?

As a strategy for gaining more confidence and positioning yourself for future promotions, the more you push yourself outside your comfort zone in each role, the more confident and uniquely valuable you will become.

So continuously seek ways to enrich your experience and present a track record that sets you apart from your peers – even if notionally you all have the same title. At the junior levels, my advice is that you try to gain breadth of experience. A 6- or 12-month rotation in another functional department will broaden out your experience and curriculum vitae. For example, a marketing analyst would enrich their marketing skills as well as their curriculum vitae by doing a six-month rotation in the sales field. Or a sales manager would benefit from serving six months in a customer service centre. If you cannot engineer a rotation to another department, then find other ways to increase the scope of your knowledge rather than stay too specialised in one niche area. For example, participate in or initiate cross-functional projects.

Although your company may want specialisation early on, it can prove detrimental to your longer-term career. After all, the only way up in corporate life is eventually into leadership positions and this means the broader your knowledge base on different functional areas, and the better your ability to manage people, the more valuable you are versus those with specialist expertise. Think about how you can gain more leadership experience in each role. If you

think about how you can gain more leadership experience in each role

want more senior roles long term, then you need to make the move to managing others as soon as possible. Try to work on a project or initiate a project which requires you to have someone more junior working for you. From having one person working for you (whether hard line, or dotted line, or just temporary project), increase the scope of the project so that you now have two people working for you. When you have one or more people working for you, it means you are gaining managerial experience whether or not your title is yet 'manager'. The more senior you become, try to ensure you get more breadth of leadership expertise – i.e. managing a larger-size team, managing a diverse team, managing multiple teams, managing remote teams.

Table 5.4 Differentiation

HOW TO GET DIFFERENTIATED
Think about the norm in your peer set, and then seek out new roles and responsibilities that will set you apart from the pack.
When you are junior you should seek to be functionally expert and functionally differentiated.
For example, if you work in Marketing, volunteer to take a six-month rotation in Sales. This kind of frontline experience will set you apart from 'ivory tower' marketers at promotion time.
When you are senior you should endeavour to gain more differentiation in the leadership space.
For example: by leading cross-functional teams/initiatives; by having a reputation as a great coach or mentor; by managing larger groups of people.

2 Tame your inner critic

We can be our own worst critics. That voice in your head telling you to do better could be your mother or father or teacher or other person of influence, who always asked you what happened to the other 10% when you got 90% in a school exam. Sound familiar? Most ambitious people are over-achievers, always dissatisfied that they are not good enough, and have not succeeded – or

most ambitious people are over-achievers

worse, feel like a failure no matter what they achieve. Try to tame your inner critic. Don't let it control you. Don't let it take away from your enjoyment of current success, and chances of future success. That other voice in your head, the calm one, the one that says 'you are good enough' – nurture that one instead!

BE POSITIVE ABOUT YOUR PROSPECTS

Optimism helps strengthen confidence levels. You will automatically feel more confident when you have taken stock of your unique value proposition for promotion. You will feel more certain about your self-worth in relation to the desired promotion. Your confidence will be grounded in substance. You will have a greater awareness of your abilities, appeal and what you have to offer. A candidate who is more certain about himself has a deeper feeling of self-worth which informs all his actions and behaviours. Add in a positive mindset and you are all set!

Optimism and resilience go hand in hand. By being positive about your promotion prospects, you continue to fire up

optimism and resilience go hand in hand

your inner resolve, and you more determinedly work through any obstacles, challenges or negativity that comes your way.

Forgive your mistakes

Deal with your mistakes appropriately. We all make mistakes. Don't keep going back over the mistake. Think instead about what lesson you need to learn, commit to trying better next time, and move on. It happened, and you can learn from it, but don't stay stuck in self-punishing thoughts about it. A very good technique for dealing with your mistakes is to practise self-compassion. Think about what your best friend or partner would say to you about what happened. Perhaps they would empathise that you were under pressure from lack of sleep, or that you did not have the experience to handle that particular situation. Through the real or imagined 'best friend' remarks, be kind to yourself, then step back and rationalise to yourself what happened and why, then learn the lesson and move on.

Go for it!

It takes courage to put yourself forward for a big role. Yes, it is exciting, but of course it is daunting too. Late at night, you start to question yourself. Can I really do it? But go with the mantra that nothing ventured is nothing gained. Taking a risk is about stepping outside your comfort zone. Do you really want to sit comfortably for the rest of your career – or do you want to really go for it and see how far you can get? **taking a risk is about stepping outside your comfort zone** I had a client who faced this very dilemma. He had a good job running a Customer Care centre. He reported directly to the Chief Executive so he sat on her management team. Having never had the opportunity to attend university, but having worked his way from the bottom up, surely getting a role reporting to the CEO was a sign of success in itself and he could rest now. Yes, of course, but I pointed out to him that he had the potential to go all the way and become a CEO himself. I was articulating something that he had more or less ruled out, because of his lack of confidence. Now that the possibility was being openly discussed, he really felt the dilemma. Enjoy his current level of success and play more golf at the weekend, or really focus and commit to going further forward? The thing is that once the idea is out of the box, it is hard to ignore it. He started to feel more confident that he could do a CEO role, and in the end it was hard to just give up on his potential, so he went for it. He got promoted to Sales Director and – eventually – CEO.

Advice from the top

Know what it is that you are aspiring to. Understand the requirements of the role and what it takes to be successful in that capacity. Be an honest evaluator of your current position, and your current capacity and capability to perform in the role that you ultimately aspire to be in. Then you need to think about how you address the gaps in your portfolio through development, through other assignments, through your own efforts to improve your skills and competencies and execute those activities along a timeline and plan.

Imagine the goal to be presenting your CV to the hiring manager or group leaders and having them examine it and see that every conceivable skill and personal quality for the target role exists within your experience set. If you treat it with that kind of thought, preparation, planning and process, your potential for success and personal satisfaction is ultimately much greater. When there are pathways available to you externally and you feel like you've maximised your prospects within an organisation – but you think you can do more – you must by the nature of the situation take a risk to glean the opportunity you want.

Focus on the outcomes that you are looking for – the opportunity for fulfilment is equally greater and thus the risk is balanced off.

BILL ARCHER, MANAGING DIRECTOR,
EIRCOM BUSINESS

Don't limit yourself to one role or one position. Your next role can be somewhere or something that you didn't expect. Don't listen to people if they tell you that you are not good enough or you have to wait. Trust yourself, that you're good enough to do this. Use your career history to give you confidence, and identify the skills that you need to develop.

DAVID HULSENBEK, HEAD OF HUMAN RESOURCES,
ABN AMRO PRIVATE BANKING INTERNATIONAL

Confidence is important – but you need to have a balance. It's important to have the belief in yourself, but don't let that come out as egotistical to your stakeholders. Get the balance right. Build credibility with your track record and don't over-think the politics – use your network and manage your stakeholders. And finally, make your ambitions known. How can you move up if no one knows your ambition?

JACQUELINE MCNAMEE, MANAGING
DIRECTOR UK, AIG

There are two fundamentals for getting to that next level: 1) tenacity and drive, and 2) self-confidence. These need to be developed. If you are knocking on the door of the C-suite, you are going to have the skills and the track record. At this level, it's about collaboration: build relationships. Take time to get feedback, speak to your stakeholders, listen and understand. You need to be delivering in your current role. You need to be knocking the ball out of the park. Think about how you are helping others and contributing beyond your own role. Think and act at the level above. Ask yourself: 'Am I demonstrating I can take on something larger?'

JOHN HARKER, CHIEF HUMAN RESOURCES
OFFICER, AL-FUTTAIM

3 Your key task: develop your value proposition for promotion

Your task now is to figure out what you have to offer the organisation if you were appointed into the next desired role. Your unique value proposition is your personal net worth on skills, track record, strengths and any other relevant value that you are bringing to the promotion.

This exercise of cataloguing your unique value proposition will give you the self-assurance and self-confidence and personal power necessary to project the right kind of energy for promotion. Once you can clearly articulate your value proposition, you will strengthen your resolve and become more confident. You can also use your unique value proposition as a way to write your curriculum vitae as part of your pitch for the role.

MY UNIQUE VALUE PROPOSITION FOR PROMOTION

With the desired promotion in mind, write down your relevant experience and ability. Try also to spot any gap areas, so that you can plan to resolve.

UNIQUE VALUE PROPOSITION	EVIDENCE
Track record:	List your performance achievements/ outcomes to date using any 'from…to' transition examples, and any rotations or people leadership highlights:
	For example: '7 years proven track record in Sales: from individual contributor to sales manager leading team of 10 for past 4 years. 6-month rotation experience in customer care centre. X% increase in sales revenue achieved by team over past 12 months under my leadership.'

▶

UNIQUE VALUE PROPOSITION	EVIDENCE
Proven ability to operate at next level up:	Provide examples of extra responsibilities under way in current role:
Strengths:	List your key strengths, with examples:
Spike: (i.e. unique talent)	Describe your spike, with examples:
Differentiation:	Explain why you stand out from your peers, with examples:

If you are asked to formally submit a biography or curriculum vitae for the promotion opportunity, I suggest you write your document using this unique value proposition template rather than a traditional format. The headers alone will demonstrate to your decision-makers how much you have thought about your net worth and the evidence underneath will provide the substance.

6

Politics: stack the odds in your favour

- Learn to read the organisation
- Build influence and leverage
- Your key task: understand the politics of your promotion

1 Learn to read the organisation

Politics are an everyday reality in the workplace and no more so than when managers are jostling competitively for a promotion.

capability alone will not be enough to get you promoted

Capability alone will not be enough to get you promoted. In order to stack the odds in your favour, you will also need to be able to read the promotion politics of your organisation.

Think about reading the organisation in terms of what is being said 'above the surface' and what is happening 'below the surface'. For example, your human resources department may explain to you the formal process of how to get promoted, and it will be important to understand that, as usually this is adhered to by timeline if nothing else. However, a recent promotee from your former peer-set might be able to give you the best insight into how the promotion decision was really made. He may tell you that there were a number of promotion criteria set out but, in the end, it came down to the bias of one influential decision-maker. Then you know that this is a critical relationship you need to build if you want to get noticed and promoted.

Table 6.1   Learn to read the organisation

THE PROMOTION PROCESS:	
Above the Surface	**Below the Surface**
The process according to your human resources department	Make your own observations: Try to decode any patterns behind the success of fast-risers in this company. Ask recent promotees how it really worked versus the official process. In the end, what really mattered, and who really mattered?

THE PROMOTION PROCESS:	
Above the Surface	**Below the Surface**
Your boss decides	Think about other possibilities: Does the team have a big influence on the decision? Who is the budget-holder? Is it your boss's boss who really decides? Have you picked a winning boss? What is your boss's career plan?
The best person always gets promoted	The 'best' person may be too valuable to promote. Never make yourself indispensable to your boss if you want a promotion: Find your successor early
Promotion is mainly about performance	Promotion is mainly about people: Play nice It's a small world
Work hard and you will get promoted	Work smart and you will get promoted: Build a strong team Demonstrate your leadership potential Position yourself for future growth opportunities
Wait for annual promotion rounds	Be opportunistic

WORK OUT THE REAL PROMOTION PROCESS

According to your human resources department

Find out what HR says is the process for promotion, as you need to know the apparent set of criteria and standards, and the timelines for the decision. The process is often outlined as involving a longlist (i.e. the total number of suitable candidates per promotion opportunity) and a group of decision-makers who work their way through a longlist set of candidates to the set of shortlisted candidates by certain dates, eventually leading to the final decision on who gets the promotion. With these formalities understood, your job is now to figure out how it really works.

Try to decode the patterns behind who gets promoted here

Make observations about the fast-risers in your company. Ask them to share their stories. Are there any common behavioural traits or interesting patterns behind their promotion success? Who and what appears to get rewarded here? What opportunities are there to emulate what you discover about how others got ahead?

make observations about the fast-risers in your company

Talk to recent promotees

The best way to emulate the fast-risers is to talk to recent promotees. Quiz them on how they got the job. Usually promotees are very frank and happy to give insights because they have already made it, plus they have recent first-hand experience of the process hoops they had to jump through and get what really mattered in the end. Try to elicit views from three or more people to start to make your own observations of any important patterns such as what really matters and who really matters at promotion time.

ARE YOU SURE YOUR BOSS DECIDES?

In lots of cases there is no need to feel overwhelmed by the politics of stakeholder management if it is simply that your current boss makes the promotion decision. When the boss decides who he wants on his team, he will usually get his way. Realistically, who is going to argue with the boss if he is passionately backing a particular candidate? Of course others are going to agree. However, the boss doesn't always make the decision, even when he says he does. So think again. Consider other possibilities:

the boss doesn't always make the decision, even when he says he does

Does the team have a big influence on the decision?

The boss may not appoint a candidate who is polarising. It is difficult to appoint someone when other team members don't rate the person and voice this view. In that instance, the boss may be faced with a rebellion in his team and have to think twice about his preferred candidate. The lesson here for you is to try to get on with everyone, and don't alienate people on your career journey. It may come back to seriously bite you on promotion rounds if you just please your boss but are a nightmare for your peers and juniors. You don't have to please everyone all the time, but you need to be a reasonable person to deal with most of the time. You can be reasonable and still be challenging, and enter into constructive conflicts, but you also need to know how

you can be reasonable and still be challenging

to repair relationships afterwards so that there are no lasting resentments or bitterness that come back to haunt you later.

Who is the budget-holder for the position?

Are you sure your boss is the decision-maker, even when he says he is? Perhaps it is his budget-holders who actually make the decision on promotions. It is worth trying to find out whether it is your boss's boss, or another budget-holder who really makes the decision. Or, if you think you can't find this out, then at least start to nurture the relationship with your boss's boss so that you are known to him and make a positive impression, further putting on the pressure for a positive result.

Does your boss's boss decide?

The 'grandparent' relationship is the relationship between you and your boss's boss. This can be a very valuable relationship in helping you to get noticed, and also loosening the control that your boss may have on you. It empowers you in your relationship with your boss if you have a good relationship with his boss. People allow themselves to get hemmed in by their boss, and

don't be afraid to build a relationship with your boss's boss

are unconscious willing participants of the control and limits that their boss places on them. Don't be afraid to build a relationship with your boss's boss. Have the courage to widen your network in the hierarchy. Take any opportunity at meetings to introduce yourself, or get into their diary.

Your boss should not find an introductions meeting with his boss objectionable. However, if your boss is insecure enough to feel anxious or threatened by this, there is a diplomatic way of managing your boss – let him know when the meeting is taking place and give him the option of joining the meeting. If your boss is mature, they won't feel threatened by you expanding your network. If your boss is immature and insecure they will feel less threatened if they know they are invited to the meeting. If your boss tells you or encourages you to cancel the meeting, don't cancel the meeting. Don't let your boss control you. You are a free agent, and need to start acting like one if you want to climb the corporate ladder. If you work in an environment where meeting your boss's boss is very unusual, then I encourage you even more so to go for it. You need to stand out from the crowd and put yourself forward as someone who is not afraid to build senior relationships. The first meeting can be introductory and include an update on your role and responsibilities. Ask your 'grandparent' what his priorities are, and how you can link your role to the achievement of those priorities. Perhaps you could also volunteer to take part in an initiative on their agenda. Take any opportunity to praise your boss or find a way to make him look good. Afterwards, always update your boss on what happened at the meeting and especially let them know what you said in praise.

Have you picked a winner boss?

If we agree that it is usually your boss who decides, then how can you pick a great boss from the get go and make your promotion prospects more favourable? Take notice of the high flyers at the next level up. If it is not your current boss, then perhaps it is one of his peers who – according to the grapevine – is more likely to get promoted at that level. If so, can you build a working relationship with that person, so that when they get promoted they would consider you for their team?

take notice of the high flyers at the next level up

Some may call this strategy 'riding on someone else's coat tails', and others may just regard you as clever for picking out who your investment bet is in terms of who has great leadership potential and will need someone loyal at their back.

What is your boss's career plan?

If your boss seems ambitious to go all the way, and is succeeding fast, then this is great news for you. However, there are dangers to limiting yourself to one boss. What if he gets fired because he overstepped the mark, or he delays his own career prospects due to personal issues such as his family don't want to relocate, or he simply plateaus at a certain point. My advice is that, as early

try to discuss your boss's career plan with him

as you can, you should try to discuss your boss's career plan with him. There would be nothing wrong with saying that you are interested in how he views his career path, so that you can gain some wisdom in terms of how to advance your own. With such a level of sharing, you might be able to anticipate where you stand and it can act as an advance heads up if things shift. For example, if your boss decides to join another company, he may give you the confidential heads up to get ready to apply for his role.

If you secured your promotion by joining a new company, then it is vital during your recruitment process that you try to work out your boss's career plan. There is a big danger that if he leaves within 6 to 12 months of your joining, you would be cast adrift in a new organisation with no sponsorship. As early as possible in the hiring process, ask your boss to be honest with you and tell you whether he intends to leave the organisation within 12 months because it will have repercussions for you. There is also an upside to having the discussion in that it may work to your advantage if you can join the company on a promise to be his successor if he chooses to leave within a year.

ARE YOU TOO VALUABLE TO GET PROMOTED?

Don't get so excited by your current role that you forget to think about your overall career game plan. Although you will want to impress your boss, you don't want to self-sabotage your career by focusing on how to please your boss to the point that they will never want to move you on. If your boss can't manage without you, then he is unlikely to ever support your move to another part of the company. I think the best way to think about succession is to shorten how long you expect to do your role. Try not to stay in any role for longer than three years. Keep this in mind right from the start, and then you have more heightened awareness of the reality that the role will end. In year one, focus on proving yourself in your current role. In year two, start to set your sights on what's next. In year three you need to be planning and negotiating your move. As part of planning your move, you need to have a successor identified by end of year two, and delegate more and more to that person during year three.

Table 6.2 A three-year horizon

THREE-YEAR ROLE HORIZON: TRY NOT TO STAY MORE THAN THREE YEARS IN THE SAME ROLE	
Year 1	Focus on proving yourself in the current role.
Year 2	Keep delivering in current role and start to set your sights on your next role. Identify your potential successor by end of year two in role.
Year 3	Delegate more responsibility to your potential successor. Plan and negotiate your next move.

PROMOTIONS ARE MAINLY ABOUT PEOPLE, NOT ABOUT PERFORMANCE

Play nice

In the end, organisations are very interpersonal places. Getting ahead is less about process, and more about the people around you. You will have an easier life, and a faster career trajectory, if you do good work, have a pleasant outlook and don't alienate anyone along the way. Playing nice doesn't mean being a people pleaser. It just means that you manage your relationships, even the challenging ones, in a reasonably healthy way – trying, as much as possible, to return them to neutral following any contentious disagreement. Of course, you cannot control the reactions of others to you and you may be called 'too smooth', 'too charming', 'too arrogant'. But if you can be pleasant even to your 'enemies' it can be quite disarming, and is better than engaging in all-out war, when inevitably both sides have so much to lose.

getting ahead is less about process, and more about the people around you

It's a small world

It can be surprising how you may find yourself continually bumping up against the same people in your company or industry, even years after you first worked with them. Really it should not be a surprise because you are both working in the same shared domain of interest. They will have formed an impression of you when you were a graduate, or a junior manager, or when they had that 'fight' with you over whether marketing or sales should get more budget. Years later, they may be the one who gets to influence your hiring decision, or decide your promotion at a new division of the company. So if this is the moment that they remember their impression of you when you were younger, then you don't want it to have been a negative experience. Wise advice is to enter freely into constructive conflict when necessary, but always find the time after the dust has settled to repair the relationship. Otherwise it is like an open wound that never healed and you may regret it later.

Advice from the top

Deliver great things, build relationships and be loyal. Let me elaborate on that. Delivering great things is different to doing a good job, but also be very clear about what your accomplishments are and what your track record is – both in terms of the narrative of your career progression and the accomplishments. Secondly, build relationships – not when you need them, but before you need them. Make sure that you have a network that provides you with opportunities. Invest in building your network, and give back to the members in that network, in a non-transactional way. Thirdly, loyalty translates into solid relationships and people who will champion you. The other thing I would add is serendipity, you know rather than having a career plan that's cast in stone, you have to be able to be agile and take advantage of opportunities when they present themselves.

ARIEL ECKSTEIN, MANAGING DIRECTOR, LINKEDIN

WORK SMART AND YOU WILL GET PROMOTED

Build a strong team

You would have started off your career at the bottom, as an individual contributor. All the emphasis from your performance appraisals was on how you needed to work hard to prove your worth. When you start managing a team, you try to get the most out of other people. However, under pressure to meet tight organisation deadlines, the manager usually still has to work at a detailed level to pick up any slack or lack of resource on the team. Sometimes it is just easier to fix problems yourself than have to constantly train up others. But, of course, this is not good for you in the longer term.

You need to delegate and get others working for you. If you are too much in the detail and working too hard on fixing all the problems, then you get stuck and can't move upwards. You need to work smarter, not harder. By stepping back from the detail,

you need to delegate and get others working for you

and investing time in recruiting the right people for your team, and investing sufficient time in training them up, your team should be doing the work for you – and you also create more time and space for yourself to think more strategically about your next move.

Demonstrate leadership ability

With emphasis early on in your career on specialist skills rather than general management skills, you will have become a subject matter expert in your area. During the early years your promotions and pay rewards will be geared towards your specialist knowledge. However, as I mentioned already, promotion is about the path to leadership, so if you want to keep getting promoted you need to remember that the end goal is to become a leader – so it is never too early to demonstrate your leadership potential. If not yet in a formal management or leadership position, you could still take the initiative to volunteer to lead particular projects for your boss, or ask for extra people responsibilities, or bring new ideas to the table that solve problems for your boss. By demonstrating leadership ability early on, you will be noticed – more so, than continuing to focus effort on just working harder and harder on the day job. Keep your focus on moving up, and don't get lost in the status of being a subject matter expert to the detriment of your next promotion.

Position yourself for future growth opportunities

Working smarter means staying alert to what growth opportunities exist. Your company will always be considering opportunities to grow and expand. If you are on more heightened alert to find out where the organisation is placing its investment bets, then you can follow the money so to speak. If you hear that the company intends to grow into a new market or launch a new product, or acquire a company, or whatever it is that will be the new buzz in the company, then try to position yourself with a role on the team responsible for investigating or delivering on the opportunity. By getting close to the action you can find out what role opportunities might exist, and if you were part of the initial investigating team then you have more knowledge than anyone else and are best placed to put yourself forward for the role. I like the saying 'fish where the fishes are', because

you need to be putting yourself in the centre of the action

quite simply you need to be putting yourself in the centre of the action, where all the resources are being invested, so that your star can rise alongside the company's growth opportunities.

BE OPPORTUNISTIC – DON'T WAIT FOR ANNUAL PROMOTION ROUNDS

If you wait for annual promotion rounds to put yourself forward for promotions, then you are putting yourself at a major disadvantage – because this is when the competition for promotion is most intense. Instead, try to get a promotion outside the normal process. Do what you can in between promotion rounds, to suggest a new role, to volunteer to run a big project, to take a role overseas or in a new division, or manage a cross-functional team, or whatever creative ideas you can spot to advance without waiting for the annual HR process. At a minimum you position yourself better by the time the annual promotion round kicks off, but hopefully you won't even need to rely on it. Please don't get institutionalised into thinking there are no exceptions to the rules. No matter what people say to you, there are always exceptions. Anything is possible. Be that exception to the rule.

Advice from the top

Just doing your job doesn't cut it and won't get you promoted. You need to show how you are driving effective change and impact over and above your role. Creating change often involves how you engage with others across the business to win support. While many try to avoid politics, the reality is that you need to become an expert in navigating politics rather than avoiding – you must learn this as a life skill. Every business has politics, even those that say they don't. The key to this skill is to approach people, decision-maker or influencer, with the best intent, be respectful, rely on the facts and then taking the emotion out of it when you are making a case. Avoid causing friction with your interactions by choosing your words and actions carefully and leaving blame out of it.

Essentially, keep it professional. Be cognisant of the fact that the leadership pyramid gets smaller as you move up – both inside the organisation and outside it in the industry. Word gets around and you need people on your side, vouching for how you operate. It's a muscle that I still work on daily.

MICHAEL KLEEF, DIRECTOR OF
AUDIENCE MARKETING, MICROSOFT

2 Build influence and leverage

By influence and leverage, I mean what bargaining power can you build with the organisation to get the promotion you desire?

The organisation needs a very good reason to promote you and not someone else. Your value proposition may be very attractive and quite nicely aligned with what the organisation values in you, but often the tipping point on promotion will be what extra leverage you have within the organisation beyond your strengths and spikes. After all, the only reason to promote you is if the organisation needs you at the next level. You may feel that you have earned a promotion, but if the organisation doesn't have a need for you at the next level up, it doesn't matter. Junior people especially do not seem to grasp this point. Promotion is not all about you, and what you have or have not done to deserve it.

promotion is about the organisation and what the organisation needs from you

Promotion is about the organisation and what the organisation needs from you. Organisations are businesses. They are in the business of making money, and you are more expensive if they promote you. You also join the narrower pool of future promotees so you need to be a good choice for the longer term beyond this role as well. The organisation needs a very good reason to promote you, and they need to feel that they will get a return on their investment in the short and long term. So what is it about you that the organisation values enough to promote you, would pay extra for, and would fight to keep you if you were unhappy?

Be mindful about the power play between yourself and the organisation when it comes to promotion rounds. It can see-saw from year to year. For example, for certain promotion rounds, you may have very little bargaining power as you may be 'desperate' for the experience that the promotion brings. Whereas in a future promotion round, perhaps you are now so established in that domain of expertise that they don't want to lose you, but would be happy to reward you with a promotion by expanding the role to include other responsibilities or markets. For example, if emerging market experience is of interest to your organisation and you have spent three years as General Manager of Middle East, you may have good leverage to bring Africa markets under your remit as a way to expand your role and secure a promotion. However, if you want to be General Manager of a more mature market such as Europe, then you will not have as much leverage to negotiate the terms of the promotion. Try to gain an understanding of the see-saw relationship of personal power and organisation power, and where that power lies for you at any particular time.

Table 6.3 Build leverage and influence

WHAT BUILDS INFLUENCE AND LEVERAGE FOR PROMOTION	WHAT DEPLETES INFLUENCE AND LEVERAGE FOR PROMOTION
Consistency of results and behaviour. Ability to manage expectations.	Missing agreed business targets. Worse still, not managing expectations.
A blend of experience to suit the growth opportunities of interest to the organisation.	Experience in an underrated or declining part of the business.
Being highly networked.	Not being well known.
Being popular with peers.	Hubris, arrogance.
Having options.	Threatening to resign. Turning down a promotion.
The right timing – getting lucky.	Asking for promotion at the wrong time.
Being in a community of interest, e.g. female, LGBT, ethnic minority.	
Having a great reputation.	Being associated with failed projects, or any other reputational weaknesses that can pull you down.
Aligning yourself with the CEO agenda on change and growth areas.	Being unaware of what the company strategy is, not knowing the names of the CEO and executive leadership team, not knowing about the big business issues of the day.

Let's go into more detail on some of the points highlighted in the table.

THE IMPORTANCE OF CONSISTENCY

Organisations need to deliver to their shareholders quarter by quarter, year by year. There is no room for error and unwanted surprises when it comes to projecting business targets because the press and shareholders can be merciless if targets are not met. So, although the organisation says it wants leaders to innovate, perhaps what it really wants is reliability from its executives. Being called a 'safe pair of hands' is a high compliment, especially in times of economic uncertainty.

BEING HIGHLY NETWORKED

By investing in your network early on, you empower yourself to find out about more opportunities for promotion. People lead to people, and promotions. Put yourself out there, build your network and build up a reservoir of loyalty and goodwill that will serve you very well when it comes to future decisions on your promotion. **invest in your network early on**

BEING A MEMBER OF A COMMUNITY OF INTEREST

An example of passive leverage is when organisations decide to set targets to promote more females or ethnic minorities into leadership positions. This is automatic promotional leverage to be more positively discriminated during senior promotion rounds. In some global firms, all female managers eligible for promotion to managing director are automatically put on the shortlist unless there is a strong case for taking them off the list.

If you fall outside a community of interest, the areas where you can more actively create leverage might be by bringing your unique skill set to a market which doesn't usually have access to your level of skill, and in return you get something extra which positions you better for promotion. For example, as a marketing director you could negotiate to take up a role in a smaller geography that really values your high level of marketing skills, so much so that they will actually give you a Commercial Director role which means you are now also responsible for the sales force. Not only do you get a promotion from Marketing Director to Commercial Director, but you are now also nicely positioned for a next promotional move into General Management.

ALIGNING YOURSELF WITH CHANGE AND GROWTH AREAS

Being politically savvy requires an ability to read the organisation context, and work it to your advantage. An example of this is when big change is about to occur. Very often we resist change, but in the context of spotting opportunities for a promotion, an upcoming merger or a new operating model is the best news you could receive. Treat change like your best friend in terms of how it represents an opportunity for you to

treat change like your best friend

move to the next level. Get involved in any committees or cross-functional teams who are doing any initial scoping of how the change will occur and when. This provides you with the inside information in advance on new organisation structure, roles required and timescales. You could potentially get involved in shaping a new required role which suits your talents, so that you are seen as part of the solution.

DON'T EVER THREATEN TO LEAVE

Your biggest leverage is to be a value-adder to the point that the organisation or your boss is anxious that you might resign. You need to play this point with subtlety. Don't ever threaten to leave in case they call your bluff. Don't ever moan about how much you could be paid elsewhere as this rubs people up the wrong way. Junior people make this mistake all the time. They think that they should let their boss know how much they could get paid elsewhere. A tactic like this is unsophisticated and you will come across as immature. No one feels good about this approach and it is always hard to recover loyalties and trust when threats enter into the debate. Instead be subtle and expand your external network and let your boss know that you are meeting interesting people in the industry. This is a subtle way of communicating that you are highly networked and have options.

HUBRIS, ARROGANCE

It can happen that you are doing a great job, you get lots of praise and you start to think how much they need you around here. A level of hubris sets in and you may think you are value-adding to the point of being invaluable. In reality no one is indispensable. A good example of this is when it comes to the time to appoint a new Group CEO. There are usually two if not three good internal **no-one is** succession candidates, all of whom are **indispensable** serious contenders for the role with excellent track record and great value-add. However, when only one of the candidates makes it, then the other two usually resign and/or may even be moved on by their new boss. This seems like a huge waste of talent, and it is, but it happens. So make sure you grow your value-add within an organisation, but also stay connected to the outside world – to your industry and your network outside the company. This provides you with other choices if your organisation chooses not to recognise your talents and you end up taking your value elsewhere.

THE RIGHT TIMING – GETTING LUCKY

Be ready to spot the opportunity when it arises. I had a young leader client whose dream role was to join the C-suite at the top of his function. Luck played a major element in getting him the promotion he wanted. When the current incumbent vacated the role, my guy got his job for a few good reasons – but one of them was because the previous year the company had gone through a reorganisation, where all the big guns had been reassigned roles, and as such it would have to be a younger leader who could fill the vacancy. A perfect storm of hard work, meets opportunity, meets luck. My client got a major leapfrog promotion, and was catapulted into the C-suite and executive leadership team.

SHOULD YOU EVER TURN DOWN A PROMOTION?

Yes, you could turn down a promotion but be absolutely clear with your stakeholders about why you are turning it down, and explain that it is a one-off for specific reasons, and it certainly doesn't mean you are not ambitious about future promotions. I think it would be a serious mistake to turn down a second consecutive opportunity. But, if you have no choice, then take great pains to be clear on your reasons and set out your timeframe for future opportunities. Let me illustrate the point with an example. A senior female executive decides to turn down a promotion because it would involve too much time away from her young **set out your timeframe for future opportunities** child. This is a common and valid reason for turning down a promotion. However, the female executive should provide a timeframe for when she would be more open to a future promotion. For example, she could say that in three years the child will be at school, and this would be a better time for expanding her career. Otherwise, if another two years go by, and the female turns down another promotion for the same reason, without communicating a future timeline, then guess what, people will start to get annoyed with what is now seen as a lack of commitment and will assume that she is never available for promotion. You are responsible for managing your own message and don't think that everyone else will work out where your head is at. You need to communicate clearly what your reasons are and what your timeframe is.

HAVING A GREAT REPUTATION

You should pay attention to how you actively build and maintain and – if necessary – repair your reputation. How others perceive you is very important to your promotion prospects because some decision-makers will actively seek views on you from a wide range of people – previous bosses, members of your team, former and current peers. When they phone colleagues to ask about you, it will be to seek a view on a general impression of you – are you reliable, can you deliver under pressure, are there any watch outs, what words would best describe you? This rolled up impression of you can make or break you at promotion time. Any unhelpful labels attached to you can stick in organisational memory for years, so you need to be aware of how others perceive you and proactively manage that view. If you think the perception of you is an underestimation of your potential – then it is up to you to change that.

Rather than assume that folks will notice the quality of your work, you need to speak up about your successes. You should let people know what you have achieved, and communicate your successes outside your 'nuclear' family as well. Take opportunities to let people know in the broader organisation that you were the one who had that great idea, or you were the one who solved that tricky problem, or managed that critical project, or whatever it was. You can do this subtly and not necessarily shout from the rooftops – but either way, make sure other people know what you are good at and what you have delivered.

make sure other people know what you are good at and what you have delivered

It is often said that women do this least effectively. The generalisation is that men are very natural at talking up their successes, whereas women are overly modest and wait for others to recognise them. So, for any reticent female readers, please know that it is not boastful or distasteful to talk about what you have achieved – it is important in the competitive corporate environment to honour yourself and your good work by letting others know about it. You don't want to end up feeling resentful that all the men are getting the promotions, even though their female counterparts are just as capable.

3 Your key task: understand the politics of your promotion

Your task is to gather political intelligence on reading the organisation, spotting opportunities to influence and building leverage towards a yes decision on you.

UNDERSTAND THE POLITICS OF MY PROMOTION	
Reading the Organisation	**Political Intelligence Gathered**
What is the real process for promotion?	
Am I sure my boss is the only decision-maker? What about his team, the budget-holder, his boss? Have I picked a winning boss? What is my boss's career plan?	
Am I too valuable to my boss to get promoted? Have I identified my successor?	
Do I place too much emphasis on performance, and not enough on people?	

UNDERSTAND THE POLITICS OF MY PROMOTION	
Reading the Organisation	**Political Intelligence Gathered**
Am I working smart versus working hard?	
Could I be more opportunistic, rather than waiting for annual promotion rounds?	
Where am I in the leverage see-saw? What can I do to build more leverage? – consistency of results and behaviour – blended experiences in line with growth opportunities – being highly networked – being popular with peers – having options – the right timing/being lucky – being in a community of interest – having a great reputation – alignment with the CEO agenda What could deplete leverage? – missing targets and not managing expectations – working in an underrated or declining part of the business – not being well known – being arrogant – threatening to leave – turning down promotions – asking for a promotion at the wrong time – being associated with failed projects – being unaware of company strategy and the key players	

7

People: figure out who makes the decision

- Identify decision-makers and influencers
- Launch your campaign
- Your key task: map your critical stakeholders

1 Identify decision-makers and influencers

Quite often it will simply be your boss deciding on your promotion. There are also plenty of scenarios where this is not the case. Make a list of all those people who could be involved in your promotion decision. This helps to map out the landscape of all possible stakeholders involved, and what connections you may need to build, renew or repair.

Consider the following:

- Who is the primary decision-maker?
- Who is the secondary decision-maker?
- Who has the power of veto?
- Who are the influencers?
- Who might want to influence against your promotion?

your main priority will be to build a good relationship with the primary decision-maker

This may seem like a lot of stakeholders. Although you need to be mindful of the role and relevance of all parties, your main priority will be to build a good relationship with the primary decision-maker, i.e. one person. Beyond that, if possible, invest your wider relationship-building campaign on about three to five people only – i.e. on the primary decision-maker, the primary influencer of the primary decision-maker, the person with power of veto and the secondary decision-maker. It is good to have a sense of the bigger picture of who might be involved, but you don't need to worry about everyone. Trust that by focusing on a few you will be investing your energies wisely.

WHO DOES THE ROLE REPORT INTO?

- Who would be your direct line boss?
- Who would be your dotted line boss?

The 'hard line' report will be the primary decision-maker.

The 'dotted line' report(s) are the secondary decision-maker(s).

Everyone else you consider important to the decision may not actually be a decision-maker, but may have importance as an influence.

WHO HAS THE POWER TO INFLUENCE THE DECISION-MAKERS?

- Incumbent team members: Who are the members of the team you wish to join, and how much influence do you reckon they will have on the decision?
- Human resources: Who is the HR partner of your new boss and how much influence will they have on the selection process and decision?
- External advisers: Are there external advisers who may be consulted? For example, the decision-maker may have a coach or an executive search adviser who may be an influence on whether to appoint an internal or external candidate.

If you are going to work for someone new, it is likely that your current boss is a major influencer because he can speak about your performance and attitude on the current job. Although his opinion will be solicited, he may not be the actual decision-maker. If you are worried that your current boss will not speak highly of you, and that he is the reason why you want a new boss, then have the courage and maturity to discuss this diplomatically with your new prospective boss. If your prospective boss hears your calm and considered version of why your working relationship with your boss broke down, you have a chance to show your maturity in the face of a relationship conflict. Your prospective boss might be impressed by your handling of the situation. Keep the explanations to a minimum and don't make it personal.

Don't list all the reasons why you can't stand your boss or why he can't stand working with you! It will make you sound like a gossip and your prospective new boss will worry that if your relationship with him breaks down, you will eventually speak this way about him too. Using a neutral tone, simply say something like, *'My working relationship with my boss broke down. We have different perspectives on how to handle situations, and all in all, it would make more sense for both of us if I were to move on.'* Only if pressed for further detail give examples, but keep

don't list all the reasons why you can't stand your boss or why he can't stand working with you!

them simple and straightforward and to a minimum, always using a neutral tone and never embellishing what happened. If you think this is unfair, and you would like to be free to air all your grievances, so that your new boss understands what you had to put up with – go ahead, it's a free country, you can say what you like – but trust me, you most likely won't get the promotion.

DOES ANYONE HAVE POWER OF VETO?

- Your boss's boss: perhaps your future boss is the decision-maker, but could his boss veto the decision in favour of another preferred candidate?

When I worked as a corporate headhunter on executive searches, this power of veto was a big frustration early on – until I learned the lesson. For months the headhunting process involved finding and selecting a shortlist of up to three candidates – only to discover at the final hour that my client's boss had a veto and, if he had not been brought along on the journey, he would raise a new issue or set out new recruitment criteria, and all three candidates could be knocked out and the search would have to start all over again. It is the same with internal promotions – get to know your boss's boss, and build the relationship as much as possible to fend off any veto scenario.

WHO MIGHT WANT TO INFLUENCE AGAINST YOU?

Hopefully no one will influence against your promotion, but don't be naive. It probably happens more often than you realise – and at all levels. There are plenty of people who think that their only route to promotion is to knock out the competition one by one. It usually happens behind your back, and the way it happens is through passive aggressive comments from your peers (who are the only ones threatened by you) and your prospective boss, and usually goes something like this:

'I love Mike. He's a great guy. But of course the thing about Mike is that he is hopeless at leading his team…'; or

'I love Sally. Everyone does … but everyone also knows Sally lacks courage to make the really tough decisions…'; or

'Matt is the best. I love working with Matt … But sadly Matt never brings a new idea to the table…'; or

'She would be a great choice … but of course she has never run a P&L before…'

This kind of sly competition is widespread. It can be very cleverly done by the masters of this subtle art of seeming to praise someone while actually knocking them out of the running. Although you possess many strengths, it is not hard for a critic to find the one obvious weakness or chink in your armour, and dial it up in their negative influencing conversations. It will also be done in such a charming way, that it won't be obvious that the critic is overtly criticising – it will be almost 'accidental' in the way it is brought up. The reason why it's clever is because they will pick a truth and run with it. So what can you do about this kind of negative campaigning? I advise you not to engage in negative campaigning yourself, and if you hear about negative campaigning against you, then you should address it head on. For example:

I advise you not to engage in negative campaigning yourself

> '… the worst someone could say about me is that I don't have the courage to take tough decisions, but perhaps that person is talking about how I behaved in the past. That was then, and this is now. I have learned since then. Recently I took the decision to <insert example> … So be in no doubt that I am ready for the promotion.'

By admitting a weakness (if true), but confining it to the past, leaves you liberated to move forward without its burden. If you are not aware of your obvious weaknesses or the negative gossip about you, it is worth asking someone on the team to do you a favour and tell you.

2 Launch your campaign

Launching your stakeholder campaign is all about courage. It might push you completely out of your comfort zone to start introducing yourself to decision-makers and asking favours from influencers. But if this is what it takes, then you need to go for it. Getting promoted is as much about your level of commitment to the process, as it is about everyone else's commitment to you. Can you really expect people to go out of their way to promote you if you won't go out of your way to get noticed? If you are willing to put yourself out there, and expand your circle of influence, then you will be one step more deservedly closer to getting the right outcome. Even if – in the end – you don't get what you want the first time, you will still end up having made new connections which will in all likelihood bear fruit in the future. By increasing your visibility, and letting people know who you are, and what your ambitions are, you exponentially increase your chances of being picked up for another promotion within the new wider sphere of possibilities created through your relationship-building efforts. Courage is about feeling the fear and doing it anyway.

courage is about feeling the fear and doing it anyway

INTRODUCE YOURSELF

I have come across cases where my client has never met the decision-maker. This is not a smart idea! You need to represent yourself and your case for promotion with the decision-makers. If you have not yet met the decision-maker, and a promotion decision is imminent, then arrange a meeting or phone call to introduce yourself. Take a moment to offer a headline or two on who you are, and what role you have, and then explain that you are one of the candidates up for promotion, and you felt it was only polite to introduce yourself. And – if the conversation is going well – perhaps you can even ask for his support. It might take guts to do it, but it really is that simple. Ignoring the decision-maker is definitely not a good idea. If there is time, getting the decision-maker onside is not a one-off meeting or transaction. It is about a more medium-term campaign over the next three or six months – depending on your timescale for promotion.

ignoring the decision-maker is definitely not a good idea

Advice from the top

The best way to influence your stakeholders is to be authentic. Tell them the reason for the conversation. Rise above the politics and demonstrate that you are not trying to manipulate them and are simply being proactive. Once they recognise your authenticity, you can move on to the next task of making them aware of what other people in the business think about your work – tell them facts – and your evidence for how you are suitable for the next level.

DR ANGEL GAVIEIRO, SENIOR VICE PRESIDENT,
FINANCIAL SERVICES

Get your visibility right. Use your success stories to make yourself visible to your key stakeholders. Most bosses will help you with that. Don't be afraid to have the conversation. Find a reason to make yourself known to people. Make what you do well relevant and use it for the conversation. You will be surprised how often the door is open. Your stakeholders understand that you want to progress and better your career. It's up to you to make your successes to date relevant to them and bring your success to them. They know it's about you, and it's about your career and enhancing your visibility – but at the same time, most will understand and respect that, and will want to help.

LAURIE BOWEN, CHIEF EXECUTIVE OFFICER
BUSINESS SOLUTIONS, CABLE & WIRELESS
COMMUNICATIONS

WARM UP THE RELATIONSHIP TO GET READY TO PITCH

If the promotion decision is not so imminent, invest your energy in warming up the relationship before you make the promotion pitch. Ask a mutual contact for advice on how to build a relationship with this person. Or you could say hello at the next company networking event, and try to find a common area of interest for discussion or further relationship-building opportunities. You could invite the decision-maker to visit your department, to sit in on a team meeting, to tour the factory floor, to meet your clients – or whatever ideas you can come up with to create some kind of connection and working relationship with your decision-maker. No matter how junior you think you are, you can implement these strategies. If you have the courage to invite the decision-maker into your working life, then you are no longer thinking like a junior person – and the decision-maker will be impressed.

WHO DO YOU KNOW THAT COULD INFLUENCE ANY OF THESE PEOPLE?

Now is the time to ask for favours from anyone who is willing to support your promotion. The more you can build a groundswell of support for your promotion, the more decision-makers will be influenced. Think about your previous bosses, even going back all the way to when you first joined the company. What senior positions do those guys hold now, and could you ask them to put in a good word for you? There is something incredibly bonding about working in the trenches on a shared goal – so much so, that even if 10 or more years go by, people who were part of the same shared team experience as you are quite likely to remember that 'nightmare' project nostalgically and may be quite happy to help you out. Anybody senior to you is not threatened by you, so these are the people most likely to help you. It gives them a sense of their own importance to bequeath favours, so everybody wins!

ASK YOUR CLIENTS TO SPEAK ON YOUR BEHALF

If you have a client-facing role, then getting a client to advocate for your promotion on your behalf can be extremely powerful. In most organisations, the customer is king, and if the customer is impressed enough to sing your praises then most likely your prospective boss will listen carefully to what they have to say. Let your client know that you are up for promotion, and ask if they would help advocate for you. If the client is not interested, then let it go, because that is their prerogative. But if the client seems amenable and agrees to help out, then perhaps you could find a valid work reason for a meeting or dinner with you, your client and your prospective boss in attendance. Fully prepped on what could be said to your prospective boss that would be helpful, your client may indeed deliver handsomely for you at the appropriate moment in the conversation. The client knows they are doing you a big favour – and hopefully, if appropriate, you can reciprocate one day.

your client may indeed deliver handsomely for you at the appropriate moment

REPAIR ANY CONFLICTS

If, within the bigger stakeholder list, there is anyone whom you have alienated in the past, then it is important that you repair this relationship. Don't simply leave it to chance that they might have forgotten how annoying you were to them or how you made them look bad in front of their boss, or whatever the conflict was about. With the passage of time, most prior conflicts can be easily reviewed in a new light and more easily forgiven. Often the easiest way to repair a relationship is to apologise for the way you behaved (whether or not you believe you behaved badly) and say that you hope it is possible to put all that behind now.

An apology can disarm the other person, especially if they were expecting more conflict. Quite likely they will say they had forgotten all about it and not to worry. Most people will react positively. If, for any reason, the person still holds a grudge, then at least you know that you tried.

an apology can disarm the other person, especially if they were expecting more conflict

GET TO KNOW THE CEO

Your trump card could be to build a relationship with the CEO – or as senior a person as possible – so that you can create great air cover from the highest office in the land. If you get on well with the CEO, then you have a lot more leverage with all the people whose job it is to keep the CEO happy. It is a lot easier than you might think to build a relationship with the CEO. The CEO usually wants to create connections at every level in the organisation – to stay in touch with the ground troops. So find out if you can put yourself forward on whatever task groups are set up to represent your level. Or think about whether there is an option for you to take the initiative to set up and lead a relevant task force that fits in with the CEO agenda, and you could invite the CEO to attend the launch meeting.

Case example

SOPHIE AND HOW SHE GOT THE ATTENTION OF HER CEO

Sophie, a Director of Sales in a US company, had just started her new role based in the European subsidiary. While she was making a good impact locally, she was very conscious of the need to build her profile in the United States where most of the senior executives

▶

operated. She was particularly keen to get on the radar of the CEO as the ultimate stakeholder.

She knew her immediate boss was a supporter already (having recruited her) but the real success lay in finding a way to impress her boss's boss, the CEO.

The CEO held an annual conference in the European subsidiary and made some key strategic statements about where the business was going. Sophie distilled the messages and made them relevant for her own team and distributed them via email. She then forwarded the email to her own boss, in the near-certain knowledge that her boss would pass them on to the CEO as an example of how this new hire thinks and how she was already adding value. The CEO, upon seeing the distilled message, was very complimentary of the email and the ability of the new hire to pick up the salient points.

The net result was that the new hire was now on the CEO radar and her boss was made to look good for hiring the right person. Everyone was a winner.

COMMUNICATE YOUR AMBITION

Start to let people know what you want. There is no point in spending all this time on nurturing these key stakeholder relationships unless you turn it into currency for your desired promotion. If that sounds quite assertive, then good. It means we are on the same page. Do you want the promotion or not?

trying to get promoted is not something to be shy about

You have to be ruthless about it. Trying to get promoted is not something to be shy about. Let people know that you are on the path for promotion and that you would like their advice and support.

Advice from the top

Show initiative, flexibility and the ability to operate on a wider scope than your current job description – you never know where in your organisation the opportunity will come from. Communicate your ambition to your stakeholders, but don't be too needy or too aggressive – this will cause you to lose gravitas. Cast your net wide and don't limit yourself to one specific role – you never know where in your organisation the opportunity will come from.

JENS BACKES, VICE PRESIDENT, ACCESS SERVICES, TELECOMS INDUSTRY

Speak to the leaders in the business and find out what they need. Meet them, let them get to know you and communicate your results and business impact. Make them aware of your ambition. Be proactive. Even if you don't think you have the capabilities, ask them what you need to do and how you can develop. Make sure people are aware that you are interested in the role even if you don't have the capabilities yet – you can develop the capabilities.

JOAN HOGAN, GROUP SENIOR MANAGER, TECHNOLOGY INDUSTRY

Don't be afraid to ask, and don't presume that you are going to get promoted. Figure out what new role matches your unique skills, and how you can solve issues for people around and above you. You've got to know what you are getting yourself into when pitching for a promotion, but don't be afraid of the things you don't know. If you have the experience, then be bullish and demonstrate how that will enable you to operate at the next level. Before you pitch, make sure you garner the right support from the right people. People who will be with you post-promotion have something to gain by it.

PETER RAWLINSON, CHIEF
MARKETING OFFICER, CONTINUITY

Be creative about how you build your relationships. Ask a key stakeholder to be a mentor, or figure out how to make a connection with them. And build the relationship. Find out what makes them tick. Take them for coffee, send them an article, play tennis with them. Build your circle and develop it.

GEORGINA FARRELL, HEAD OF
HUMAN RESOURCES, UK INSURANCE INDUSTRY

Driving change and delivery are key. You need to be known for delivery as a starting point. At a junior level, you also need to figure out exactly what you need to be delivering in order to impress. This can be company, and industry, specific. I believe the idea of being a functional director is outdated. Companies want people who can work across functions in a collaborative manner. The people who do well have the ability to work across borders. It then comes down to two things: reputation management and network. Firstly, you need to manage your reputation with the right people. Secondly, you need to be able to influence the right people, so when the opportunity comes up, the decision-maker knows you, and has you in mind for the promotion. The guy who does great work, but no one knows, will never get a promotion.

MARCUS MILLERSHIP, HEAD OF HUMAN RESOURCES,
ROLLS-ROYCE SHARED SERVICES

3 Your key task: map your critical stakeholders

Your task is to identify the decision-makers and their influencers and to start your campaign to get promoted.

1. Identify all the people involved in the promotion decision:

MAP YOUR STAKEHOLDERS	
Who will the role report into?	**Names of Decision-makers**
Who would be your direct line boss?	
Who owns the budget for the position?	
Who would be your dotted line boss?	
Who has power of veto?	
Who has power of veto?	
Who has the power to influence the decision-makers?	**Names of Influencers:**
Who are the influencers?	
Who might influence against you?	

2. Establish their priority of importance:

- primary decision-maker(s)
- power of veto
- secondary decision-maker(s)
- influencer(s)

Draw three concentric circles. In the central circle, put the name of who you assess to be the primary decision-maker and the name of anyone with power of veto over the primary decision-maker. In the next outer circle, list the secondary decision-makers. In the final outer circle, write the names of the influencers, i.e. anyone who has power to influence the primary decision-maker, the power to influence the person with power of veto, and power to influence the secondary decision-makers (see Figure 7.1).

Figure 7.1 Your role stakeholders

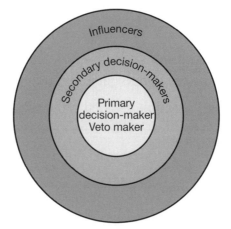

This is your list of stakeholders. But don't feel overwhelmed if that ends up being circa 10 or more people. The list usually comes with some obvious opportunities for calibration. The primary decision-maker is the key person and, often, no one else really matters as much, because the stakes may not be high enough for anyone else to disagree with the primary decision-maker.

3. Decide who is most important and launch your campaign:

MAP THE STAKEHOLDER LANDSCAPE		
Stakeholders:	**Write the names:**	**Start your campaign**
1. Primary decision-maker		Make connections:
2. Influencers of the primary decision-maker		1. Introduce yourself. 2. Warm up the relationship to get ready to pitch.
3. Person with power of veto		3. Who do you know that could influence any of these people?
4. Influencers of the person with power of veto		
5. Secondary decision-makers		4. Ask your clients to speak on your behalf.
6. Influencers of the secondary decision-maker(s)		5. Repair any conflicts. 6. Get to know the CEO. 7. Communicate your ambition.

8

Performance: deliver great results to get attention

- Establish an impressive platform of results
- Identify the next big wave
- Your key task: shape your new ideas

1 Establish an impressive platform of results

Throughout this book I have emphasised the importance of doing more than just a good job in your current role. But let's be clear, you can't lose sight of what you need to deliver in the short term. How you meet and exceed expectations in this role will be indicative to decision-makers of your future potential.

Establish an impressive platform of results

- Deliver your existing responsibilities on time, on budget
- Get your team working for you
- Offer to take responsibilities from your boss
- Work on high-profile projects
- Show leadership capability
- Take part in a cross-functional initiative
- Gain international experience early on
- Get involved with innovation projects, or set one up
- Represent your firm at industry platform events

DELIVER YOUR EXISTING RESPONSIBILITIES ON TIME, ON BUDGET

It might sound obvious, but you need to be doing a good job in your current role, to be considered for promotion to the next level up. I learned the mantra 'on time, on budget' early on in my Accenture career, and it has stuck with me. Make it yours. There is nothing more pleasing to a client, or to your boss, than a solid track record of meeting your deadlines and staying within budget.

Just remember that it's all about working smart, not hard – and free up some time to plan your next promotion. Most middle managers are too busy working on the detail, and producing results – giving little time or space to considering how to move on to the next role. I have said it a few times already, but I cannot say it enough – performance alone will not get you the promotion. On the other hand, if you are not doing a good enough job in your current role, then you are seriously hampering your prospects of being considered for something up a level.

GET YOUR TEAM WORKING FOR YOU

As part of carving out some time to focus on your promotion prospects, are there opportunities to get your team working harder for you? Is it time to reset priorities for the team and individual team members? What if you assume that you will be getting a promotion within three months, what changes would you need to put in place between now and then? You would have to find a successor. Do you have one? If not, why not? You should always have someone on the team who is capable of taking over from you. If there is someone with potential on your team, start investing in them now. If there is not someone on the team who has the potential to take over your role,

you should always have someone on the team who is capable of taking over from you

then think about the criteria you would set out for a recruitment brief and start discussing with your HR partner the need to get a number two on your team. If you feel that it would shake things up in a constructive way, then start telling people that you want to get a promotion, and are getting ready to move on.

OFFER TO TAKE RESPONSIBILITIES FROM YOUR BOSS

Ask your boss for extra responsibilities. But remember that your goal is to get promoted. Ask for responsibilities that will help

remember that your goal is to get promoted

with your leadership skills, and increase your visibility within the firm. Don't end up doing extra administrative tasks and being a martyr to your boss – making him look good, while you do all the work and get none of the reward. As you take on more leadership responsibility, you need to let your boss know that you are doing this in order to build experience in readiness for promotion. Let other people know that you have also taken on new responsibilities so that they realise you are ambitious, and that you have taken initiative. Don't be modest about your achievements.

Advice from the top

My starting point is that you need to deliver on the commitments you make in the current job. No matter how big your ambitions, don't let them distract you from excelling in your current role. You always need to take care of today's business so that nobody – peers, direct reports, or those above you – questions your performance. Secondly, treat people consistently whether working alongside them, for them, or they for you. Finally, also be conscious about the relationships you form; it's not just for the sake of being networked, it's about building long-term relationships by being genuinely interested and curious about people.

ANDREW FARMER, CIO INTERNATIONAL
FINANCIAL SERVICES, COMMONWEALTH BANK

Perform to the max for at least 6 to 12 months before promotion time. Show the ability to operate at the next level and show commercial savvy. Then you are demonstrating your value and you'll be in a position to demonstrate your worth to the business at the next level. The final part is to always show confidence.

AVRIL TWOMEY, HEAD OF MARKETING,
GLENILEN FARM, FMCG INDUSTRY

WORK ON HIGH-PROFILE PROJECTS

Do you know what matters to the CEO? What is the company strategy? What are the key projects that are trickling down from the CEO agenda? If you don't already know the answers to these questions, then now is the opportunity to find out. If you feel like the Group CEO is a million miles away from your reality, then this in itself is an insight. Why do you feel so disconnected from the CEO agenda and the company strategy? If you feel this way, it is quite likely that so do many others. Could you try to fill the void by suggesting to your boss or your boss's boss that you set up and lead a taskforce on connecting the company strategy with the on-the-job day-to-day reality? Try to either work on a high-profile change project, or set one up. Either way, try to gain visibility with the Group CEO or as **try to either work on a high-profile change project, or set one up** close as you can get to the top. It may be easier than you think. There are always ongoing organisation change projects. You just need to do your research and find out what is under way and try to play a contributing role. Start with any project that involves management consultants – if the company is willing to invest in management consulting fees then you can be sure that they are working on a strategic change initiative.

Case example

FABRICE AND HOW HE PROACTIVELY SECURED PROMOTION

Early in his career, Fabrice joined an industry-leading energy company as a Regional Business Development Manager. He was reporting to the Country Business Development Director and decided he wanted a more strategic role.

▶

After a few months, a project came up in the business which involved bringing previously outsourced business development operations in-house. Fabrice put out some feelers about the project. He soon learned that a number of key people in the business were running the project and that the CEO of the company was the key sponsor. In fact, the first briefing meeting was being given by the CEO.

Recognising the opportunity for exposure, Fabrice discussed the project with his boss. He put himself forward for the project and was appointed Project Lead. His boss advised that Fabrice use the project to build relationships with the key stakeholders. Fabrice knew that this was an opportunity to impress, and worked hard to deliver against the project objectives. Through the project, he had regular contact with a number of C-level executives and consciously raised his profile with the Group Commercial Director, sending him updates on the project.

Towards the end of the project, Fabrice received a call from the Group Commercial Director who informed him that his name had been mentioned by his boss in relation to a Country Director's vacancy in another region and asked would he like to discuss the role. Of course, Fabrice jumped at the opportunity. Fabrice interviewed for the role and was offered the job.

Within 18 months of his promotion, the company experienced a reorganisation. Fabrice was again approached, this time by the CEO, to lead a turnaround project for the business over two years. Fabrice used the opportunity to express his interest in being part of the group leadership executive team. Fabrice had a discussion with the CEO about the role, and what it would take for him to make the step up. Armed with the necessary information and using the project as his opportunity, Fabrice worked hard to deliver results. Within a further 18 months, he was on the executive leadership team reporting to the Group CEO.

SHOW LEADERSHIP QUALITY

Could you become a first among equals on your team, by demonstrating your leadership qualities to your boss? Do you think your boss considers you as his successor – and if not, why not? Could you ask your boss for advice on how you could demonstrate more leadership quality?

Is there a new practice area that you could offer to lead? If you can come up with an idea for a new growth area for the company, and create the business case for it, then you are clearly showing your leadership capability and readiness/deserving of a promotion. Demonstrate early in your career that you have the courage, willingness and confidence to make changes for the good of the business.

No matter what level you are, you can follow the advice above. Don't see it as something that you could do when you are promoted, or when you are more senior. Empower yourself to be a leader now. For example, if you are in your twenties, you will be a lot more technically savvy than some of the elders in their forties

empower yourself to be a leader now

and fifties. Perhaps you can suggest a digital strategy or a new app to enhance your company products and services.

TAKE PART IN A CROSS-FUNCTIONAL INITIATIVE

Corporations are so highly matrixed that cross-functional initiatives are necessary to improve communication and coordination of goals across various divisional teams. Participating in one such cross-functional team is a great way of getting visibility with decision-makers outside your functional area. Not only does this give you visibility and greater access to decision-makers, but you can also learn a lot from your peers in other divisions about what promotion opportunities may exist in their areas, and who is a good boss to work for.

Cross-functional initiatives are also a great way to take up an informal leadership position. Usually people are not particularly keen on leading such projects because of the time it takes away from their day job. However, you could take the view that leading a cross-functional initiative is a good investment in your leadership skills and experience.

GAIN INTERNATIONAL EXPERIENCE EARLY ON

Working in another culture can be invaluable for broadening your experience and skill set, and will pay rich dividends for your long-term career. Learning how to adapt to new cultures and new environments is a skill in itself, and something that promotion decision-makers hold in high regard. You will benefit from participating on diverse teams or from learning how to influence and lead people from a different background from yours. It can be very exciting to work in emerging markets versus more mature markets. Emerging markets, by their very definition, are where the future growth of your company lies – and, as such, will be where the promotion opportunities also exist. It is also possible to accelerate up through your career track faster into more senior positions by taking up posts in emerging markets. Find out where your company is setting up any new divisions – and consider participating.

emerging markets are where the future growth of your company lies

AOIBHE AND THE BENEFIT OF GAINING INTERNATIONAL EXPERIENCE EARLY ON

Aoibhe, now the CEO of a pharmaceuticals company, believes that the experience she gained from a two-year stint in a research and development (R&D) role as an expat in the United States early in her career was invaluable for helping her get to her current position.

Previously in her career, she had always worked in marketing and wasn't enamoured by a company request that required her to move from her home in the Netherlands for an R&D role – her passion was marketing. On top of the change of function, it involved uprooting and moving her family across the Atlantic. Reflecting on the experience now, she recognises that as well as the commitment and flexibility she demonstrated, she gained hugely from the experience of changing functions. At the time, it was unusual to gain international and cross-functional experience – so her know-how differentiated her from the rest of her peers.

Looking back with her current understanding of what it takes to lead a company, Aoibhe recognises that she implemented a good strategy. She lined up a very good successor to take on her marketing management role when she left the Netherlands. This kept her reputation intact after moving roles and showed commitment to the business. The move to the United States was her first venture into international and cross-functional experience – essential for any contemporary business leader to be able to see things from more than one perspective.

▶

Also, at the time, after being approached by her bosses about the role, Aoibhe had a moment of clarity. She realised that they had asked her for a reason: either they thought she was the best person to do the job, or they were facing a major challenge and needed someone to help. Either way, she knew it was an opportunity to impress, and to lead a project and demonstrate her ability to deliver.

GET INVOLVED IN INNOVATION PROJECTS, OR SET ONE UP

Most companies are concerned about lack of innovation, and how to embed the innovation gene within the company DNA. If there are no innovation projects in your company, then you will be regarded as creative by simply pointing this out. You could offer to set up a taskforce to investigate the future trends in your industry, and possibilities of innovations and industry disrupters, and how your company could position itself better for the future. It would only take a few hours on the internet to research what other companies do to encourage innovation. Then you could write up these best practices and present them to your boss.

REPRESENT YOUR FIRM AT INDUSTRY PLATFORM EVENTS

Most people have a big fear of speaking in public, so if you have the confidence to represent your company at industry events, then you will be able to set yourself apart from your peers. Perhaps you can start by writing a paper on a specialist topic and publishing that paper as marketing material, and then lifting out the key points to create a speech on the topic. Your marketing and communications department may welcome your initiative, and offer to position you for external speaker events.

Advice from the top

Although you have a specific role, with targets and objectives, you need to put energy into guiding, and inspiring your stakeholders. And obviously you need to deliver and underpin your potential advancement by showing results. What's interesting here – the secret – is that the way in which you set, communicate and connect your results with your management action can be as important as the results themselves.

You need to have an inspiring story to explain your priorities and the way in which you achieved the results. Explain the methodology you followed and your management style, and how these can be applicable to the next role that you want to undertake. This specific link between your achievements and the ability to transfer the skills that you are showing to something bigger really makes the difference when a potential career advancement is on the radar screen!

Really, the key is do an analysis every now and then of what brought you to a certain level in your organisation – the skills and your credibility – and recognise what can help you get to the next level. Then you need to find the courage to discard some of the things that helped you get to where you are so you can concentrate on what is more important going forward. This is very difficult, as the things you need to discard can represent a pillar for your career and are often activities you enjoy a lot. You need to stop doing things that although have been a valuable asset for your career progression so far, are no longer the most relevant activities for your current situation

> *if you really want to get a broader role in your organisation. You need to have the courage to leave those things behind – delegate if you have to – and to take the risk and expand your skill set for your next senior leadership role.*
>
> ANDREA GUERZONI, TRANSACTION ADVISORY
> SERVICES LEADER FOR EUROPE, MIDDLE EAST,
> INDIA AND AFRICA (EMEIA), EY

2 Identify the next big wave

The 'Performance' P is not just about doing a good job in your current role. I would also like you to be the person to identify 'the next big wave'. What I mean by that is there is always something new around the corner – a game changer, a disruptor, an alternative product or service, a new technology or new channel to market. Could you be the one to identify it? It would certainly catapult you into the promotion spotlight if you can be the one to spot a trend early or bring a great new idea to the leadership table.

The big wave may have already arrived, and your company is ignoring it. You can be the one to point this out: for example, if your company works in the hotel industry but is complacently ignoring the disruption caused by the new 'sharing economy' companies, who are on a massive growth trajectory by cutting out traditional service providers. Or if your company works in city transport, but is not using smartphone application technology to drive customer traffic to your services. If 'denial' is part of your company or divisional strategy, then you can be the one to call it out, and advocate for more engagement in the new reality. Be a leader, be a strategist, and be a futurist.

be a leader, be a strategist, and be a futurist

Figure 8.1 What is the next big wave?

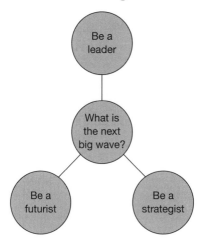

LISTEN TO CUSTOMERS

Do your customer research. Pay close attention to what your customers are suggesting or complaining about. The closer you are to the customer, the more likely you are to spot what the customer wants next. Ironically it is the more junior people who are usually on the front line and the closest to the customer – so even though you might feel too junior to

pay close attention to what your customers are suggesting or complaining about

have a view, be aware that you actually have greater access to the customer truth than the CEO and his leadership team. Be prepared to state the obvious, especially when no one else will. Most people, including your boss, the CEO and leadership team, are usually so focused on next quarter results that there is not always time for them to think about industry game changers. At the top level, there is too much attachment to how things are, and not enough focus on how things could be. You might be the one to have an insight that is better than all the rest. Let's take a simple example – supermarkets. There was a time when fresh fruit and bakeries were not sold in-store. Now we see it as commonplace. At the time this was a transformative innovation for supermarkets. So look at your company's situation and the industry you operate in, and think about its biggest problems and whether you have any creativity or insight into how to resolve.

FIND OUT WHAT THE CONSULTANCIES ARE SELLING

It is always a good idea to take a meeting with a management consultant – and especially a good idea to take a meeting with entrepreneurs. Usually consultancies have a future-forward perspective and are selling ideas and services that are not yet fully arrived or normalised. You can get educated on what's ahead by looking at the websites of the top consultancies. For example, I took a look at the big four management consultancies and noticed that there is a big spotlight on cybersecurity services. That makes sense given the recent corporate hacking scandals. But for your purposes it begs the question around whether your company is equipped to protect itself against cyberattacks. Could you imagine scenarios where cyberattacks have a massive negative impact on your business? How could you craft this topic area as a great insight for how your company could improve? Can you link it to your desired promotion role? Could you craft a promotion role as the new strategic in-house cybersecurity expert?

THINK ABOUT A WORLD OF POSSIBILITIES

Instead of thinking about what can't be done, start to think about possibilities without limitations. Reframe your mindset. For example, if I had endless resources, what could I achieve? If I had unlimited budget, what could I do? If I had a better team, what could we achieve? If I had 10% more hours in the day, what could I focus on that would be strategic? Is there another way we can achieve our goals? This might generate ideas on how to refocus and restructure you team to focus on new priorities.

USE COMPANY ASSETS TO UNLOCK MORE VALUE

Give yourself permission to be the smartest person in the room, to voice your opinion and to share your insights. The best ideas come from looking at your company assets and unlocking them to create more value. With the next big wave in mind, try to develop a new idea that either utilises the organisation's existing assets to unlock more value – or any other idea that is imaginative, creative and improves the company revenue. This will get you noticed and the organisation is more likely to invest in you.

Case example

SARAH AND THE IMPORTANCE OF DOING SOMETHING BIG

Sarah's perspective on having a great career is as follows:

> *'Always do something big'* – It's really important to find a way to be extraordinary with what you are doing, and be exceptional, rather than just trying to figure out how to make your target. This will make you stand out in a role and open lots of doors both inside and outside your company.

▶

'Know when to move on' – If you feel like you have gone as far as you can in a role or a company or under a particular boss, move on. Learn to recognise the signs, timescales and anticipate.

'Open as many doors for yourself as you can in your career' – Working in a global context opens a lot more doors. Changing industries opens doors. Changing functions opens doors.

The first of Sarah's tactics has been to deliver outstanding work and use that as a launch pad for promotion. But, isn't delivering outstanding work a base line expectation anyway? Yes it is. But I mean *really* outstanding work. Outstanding work and doing something big is about doing something different and surpassing expectations. By the time Sarah had built up 20 years' experience in the telecoms consulting industry, she had been successfully running a multimillion-dollar client account. She was given a new role managing a key account – a financial sector giant – as the previous managing director of the account was retiring. The outgoing MD had been doing a tremendous job. He'd regularly have dinner with the client's CEO, and it was a billion-dollar account that he was running really well. It was *the* most successful account in the company. Sarah recalls that she had mixed feelings about taking on the job:

> 'I knew it would be a massive challenge – I mean how do you improve on that? Billion-dollar account? Most successful account in the company? I knew if I was going to take on the job that I'd have to do something big. So we sold them something that had never been sold before. We sold them a whole network. It was high impact, and gave me visibility all over my company. It really changed everything for me.'

3 Your key task: shape your new ideas

In the context of the next big wave, what are your new ideas? If you do the research and are in a position to talk about the next big disrupter to your industry, and bring a big new idea – or set of good ideas – to your pitch for the new desired role, then you have boosted your promotion chances considerably. Even if the idea is too ambitious and would cost too much to implement, at least you have demonstrated your ability to think outside the box and be creative. Prospective bosses love someone with the confidence to bring new ideas to the table.

SHAPE YOUR NEW IDEAS	
Listen to customers: What are the customers complaining about? What are the customers asking for?	
Meet the management consultants to find out: What are the latest trends? What are the hot topics?	
Think about a world of possibilities: Use Imagination Think about the 'what ifs'? What are the possibilities? What if there were no limits? Use Curiosity Why do we do it this way? Why don't we do it another way?	
Use company assets to unlock more value: What are our core company assets? Could we use them for another purpose?	

Advice from the top

A key factor to being successful is having an impact. This means three important things to me. First of all, this is about developing an inspiring point of view that energises personally as well as the organisation. Secondly, you embed this within the organisation and give it a purpose. Last but not least, impact and success come by consistently providing authentic proof points of success! If you do this well, people will feel the energy and rally around the purpose. This then becomes your narrative and the opportunities will follow.

JAN ZIJDERVELD, PRESIDENT OF EUROPE, UNILEVER

9

Proactivity: put yourself forward for the role

- When and how to ask for promotion
- Prepare your pitch
- Your key task: write up your role vision and anticipated priorities

1 When and how to ask for promotion

Being proactive is essential if you want to get promoted. The organisation is unlikely to promote someone who doesn't have the self-confidence to put themselves forward for promotion. Dropping hints won't cut it. You need to come right out and ask for the promotion.

When and how to ask for promotion

- If you don't ask for promotion, don't expect to get it
- The importance of timing
- Don't wait for a vacancy to come up
- Don't fall down at the first hurdle

IF YOU DON'T ASK FOR PROMOTION, DON'T EXPECT TO GET IT

Of course most people would love it if their boss would wake up one day and finally spot their fabulousness and lift them up out of the obscurity of middle management. I can tell you now that this is never going to happen. By the time all the forthright people have gone and put themselves forward for senior roles, and built sufficient leverage to deserve them, there won't be any vacancies left for the polite and well-mannered folks.

in the competitive world of business, you can't hold back A lot of people think that it is too pushy to ask for a promotion. They want it to happen without having to ask for it. We don't want to be seen as aggressive or 'ill-mannered'. But while you may not be a pushy person by nature, in the competitive world of business, you can't hold back. You need to be assertive and articulate what you want. Your boss or prospective boss is not a mind-reader, and likely not so clear-sighted to realise that when a role vacancy arises on his team, you are the best choice. You have to have planted the seed in his mind already – months in advance. Then your name will swim before him in his mind, at the right time.

Case example

PIERRE AND HOW HE TOOK CONTROL OF HIS PROMOTION TO DIRECTOR

Pierre spent two years as Senior HR Manager – prior to an accelerated promotion to HR Director role in a global management consulting firm.

From early on in his Manager role he knew that he wanted to be Director – he was ambitious and he wanted his boss's job. There were seven other HR Managers who were potentially eligible for the job. On top of that, the firm often sourced candidates externally for Directors' roles if they believed that the talent was not present internally. Pierre also knew that, from the firm's perspective, he didn't have all of the required skills to be Director. He would need to undergo some leadership development in order to fit the Director profile. The biggest challenge of all was figuring out the timing of when Pierre's boss would be moving on.

So how did Pierre manage to get the Director's job?

Pierre and his boss got on well and Pierre knew that there was mutual respect between them. Pierre felt a little cheeky when he casually mentioned to his boss that he

▶

would love to have his job some day. It turned out that his boss was also an ambitious guy, and had aspirations to leave the company within the next few years for a bigger role which would leave the Director job vacant. Without promising Pierre the job, the Director agreed to help him create a plan to get promoted. After all this was mutually beneficial – Pierre would be very well positioned to get the promotion and his boss would have a credible successor.

There were three key elements to the plan agreed with his boss:

First, Pierre needed to start scoring bigger wins on performance. He had been operating effectively in a supporting role up until that point, but he needed to secure more wins for the business and communicate those successes to the executives who would be making decisions about his promotion. Pierre spoke to a select number of peers informally – a list of peers he created with his boss – to find out what these 'wins' and 'goals' looked like. He then built these into his yearly objectives via the formal company process and annual review.

Secondly, Pierre needed to demonstrate personal development and enhanced leadership skills in a number of areas – most notably in strategy. He enrolled on an intensive HR strategy course, and secured funding from the company for this. Pierre used the personal development objectives in his annual review which focused on 'demonstrating a strategic mindset and approach' to build his case to secure the funding.

Thirdly, Pierre created a stakeholder map identifying those who could potentially influence the decision on who would become the next HR Director. With the help of his boss, he identified ways to become an adviser to these stakeholders. This would allow him to demonstrate his newly acquired skills and ability to operate at 'Director-level', all the while giving him the opportunity to build personal relationships with the decision-makers.

Through a new initiative, Pierre and his boss crafted the opportunity for him to engage with the CEO on a regular basis, which provided the opportunity for him to communicate his ambition.

After about 18 months, Pierre had played a central role on a number of wins for the business and was very successfully demonstrating his ability to operate at a strategic level. But all was quiet on the promotion front. His boss was not yet ready to vacate the role for another six months. During that time Pierre continued to impress and put time and energy into nurturing his relationships. Then less than two years after creating their plan, his boss left the firm and Pierre was promoted to Director.

THE IMPORTANCE OF TIMING

The more you can tie the promotion pitch to an appropriate work context, the better. So, think about the timing opportunities ahead for you. Perhaps you could wait for the next Leadership Development or Strategy away day to make your move. Decision-makers are in a different mindset out of the office, and are especially open-minded during away days. Otherwise just be brave and set up an office meeting with the decision-maker(s) to update on your work progress. Ideally this is an update on the cross-functional initiative to which you now belong, or the Innovation Group you set up or it could just be your day job role update.

think about the timing opportunities ahead for you

It can be very hard getting into the diary of some decision-makers, and when you get that slot, you need to use it wisely. Yes, cover off the work update as promised, but keep it short and keep issues to a minimum. Then ask for advice on how to position yourself for promotion, explaining your vision for what you would do if you were promoted into the next role. If you want to give the person a heads-up that a promotion discussion would be on the meeting agenda, then this is fine too. Sometimes the element of surprise is more effective for getting an honest reaction.

I realise that most people will find this approach very brazen. Yes, it is. But do you want the promotion or not? If you do, then you have to be brazen about asking for it. I urge you to be confident enough to ask for what you want. If you feel confident about your value proposition, you will feel more comfortable asking. Trust me, in 9 out of 10 cases the person will be impressed by your confidence and ambition. In the case that they don't appreciate it, then you will know that you had nothing to lose.

DON'T WAIT FOR THE VACANCY TO COME UP

People move from roles all the time, so you need to have put your hat firmly in the ring before the vacancy arises. You can create a 'psychological contract' with the decision-maker by saying, *'If that role ever comes up, I would like you to consider me.'* There is no ambiguity. By putting it out there, you have staked a claim on that particular role. Now the decision-maker knows you will be unhappy if you don't get it. If it matters to that person to keep you from being unhappy, then it makes it harder for them not to give it to you when the vacancy arises.

you need to have put your hat firmly in the ring before the vacancy arises

If they do give the role to someone else, they are under more pressure to offer you something else to keep you happy. If they don't care about making you happy, then maybe you start to realise that you need a new boss.

There is no downside to being proactive and asking for promotion. Even if you are overreaching, and the person had underestimated you, they will admire your chutzpah and it will make them think twice about you. Just remember that your proactivity in pushing for a role needs to come with some substance as well.

DON'T FALL AT THE FIRST HURDLE

You should expect a 'No' or a 'Not Yet', when you first ask for promotion. That way you won't set yourself up for disappointment, but realise that it is a first step in your approach. The way to deal with initial rejection and discouraging tones is to expect them in advance, and be armed with a response: *'I thought you might say that, but I am committed to getting a promotion, so tell me what I would need to do or change to get there.'* Not only does that sound like a confident and mature stance, now the pressure is on the other person to explain what you need to do. This can make for great feedback. If the other person clearly spells out how you need to change, or what results you need to deliver, then you have a line of attack on where to focus your efforts going forward. Also, another 'psychological contract' ensues between your boss and you. *'I told him to do X; within six months he has done X; now I need to promote him.'*

For example, I worked with a client who wanted to move from Manager to Director. When she asked those who had been recently successful on that transition to offer their advice, they told her she wouldn't make it in less than two years. This was very discouraging because she wanted the promotion this year.

This client was so easily discouraged that she would have given up that year and simply waited for her turn to come up. This is classic institutionalised stuck mind: *'They told me it would take two years, and therefore it will take two years.'* Don't let others control you! I convinced my client that anything was possible. Just because people say it will

go for it, with gusto, and see what happens

take two years doesn't mean that you can't do it in one year. Why let others depress you? Go for it, with gusto, and see what happens. Take that first step to believe in you, and believe that anything can happen, and be proactive in making the promotion happen sooner rather than later. After all, if you believe it will take two years, and you plan accordingly, then guess what, it will take two years. If you believe it is possible to happen within one year, and you plan accordingly, then guess what, it might just take only one year.

2 Prepare your pitch

WRITE UP YOUR ROLE VISION, FIRST 12-MONTH PRIORITIES AND FIRST 100 DAYS PLAN

To back up asking for the role, it would be impressive if you have a written document that describes your vision for the role, and your first 12-month priorities if you were appointed. In this document, you might even want to include what you would hope to achieve by the end of your first 100 days in role. That level of detail will show a degree of seriousness on your side, and a level of commitment to the new role, that would really impress a decision-maker.

By 'Role Vision' I mean specific ideas on what you would want to achieve within two to three years within the role under your leadership. This is your manifesto for the role.

Your Next Role – Vision Statement

What I would like to achieve within three years on:

- Vision and strategy
- People and teams
- Results and deliverables

By 'First 12-Month Priorities' I mean the list of approximately 7 to 10 critical areas of priority that you would focus on during your first year in office. In line with the role vision you set out, where you would want to be at the end of your first year in the role in areas such as:

- delivery of the strategy
- recruitment/re-assignment of resources
- business targets
- innovation.

By 'First 100 Days Plan' I mean a list of up to 10 desired outcomes that you would want to achieve within the first three to four months of the role, demonstrating alignment to the role vision and first 12-month priorities. List what actions you would take to get off to a very fast start as the new leader in areas such as:

- managing the role transition
- securing an early win
- building the right team
- stakeholder relationships.

Your written document should be long enough to show you have thought it through, but short enough that your decision-maker will actually take the time to read it. Perhaps it would be 10 or 12 pages long. It needs exciting headers, and fresh ideas.

It's your pitch for why you should get the job, so be convincing. This is not about who you are (it's not a CV), but about what you can offer the role (your ideas, your vision for what can be achieved, your alignment with what the firm needs). The exercise of writing down your ideas as leader-in-role forces you to really think through what you can offer the company in the new role.

For example, I was working with a client who wanted to be the Group HR Director. So I assisted and encouraged her to write down on paper what she would achieve for the company, if she was appointed into the role. This document included her ideas on a new people direction for the firm, a new approach to human resources planning, and a list of options on areas of culture improvement within the company. The Group CEO was very impressed that my client had taken the initiative to pitch for the role with substance – not just verbally – and also he liked the quality of the ideas. My client hadn't realised that the Group CEO was no longer impressed with the incumbent Group HR Director and this paper acted as a catalyst for change. My client was in the new role in time for the new financial year.

Case example

SAOIRSE AND HOW SHE PROACTIVELY SECURED HER PROMOTION TO VICE PRESIDENT

Saoirse was working in a start-up tech company as a junior Product Manager in her twenties. She worked alongside a dozen or so other Product Managers. The reporting structure in the company was relatively flat, and the dozen or so Product Managers all reported directly to the CEO. Town hall sessions and meetings were often frustrating and counterproductive for all involved.

The CEO was an entrepreneur, and not tech savvy. The Product Managers would discuss the minute detail of their products, projects and the related problems and the CEO would get increasingly frustrated about the barrage of detail and lack of what he perceived to be more strategic valuable information from a dozen people. Equally, the Product Managers found the CEO difficult to approach when they needed to get sign-off, and often procrastinated about having simple discussions with him.

Saoirse, and probably some of the other Product Managers, knew that in the long term the situation was not sustainable. It was clear that the Product Managers needed a Manager who understood what they were talking about, and who could then take the top-line information to the CEO, who could make decisions based on the key information. Saoirse recognised that she had the technical knowledge, and the communication skills to do the job, but at 24 she had never managed anyone.

So Saoirse took action. She booked onto a one-day management development course. She used some of the information she learned that day to create a proposal for a new reporting structure for the team, which involved creating a new role for a VP of Product Management, who would manage the team and report directly to the CEO. Saoirse arranged a chat with the CEO and nervously sat down with him one afternoon. She showed him the document and talked through the benefits of the new reporting process, how it would make the Product Managers more productive and how it would make the CEO's life easier. The CEO calmly sat back in his chair, and said: 'I am pleased that one of you guys stepped up – I was hoping someone would! Here's what we'll do...'

▶

But Saoirse's boss didn't give her the promotion immediately. He told her to go and talk to the team of Product Managers, and find out from them if they thought that it was a good idea. If people saw value in creating a new position, then he would support the idea and make it happen. Over the next few months, Saoirse floated the idea with the team, first in informal settings and then more formally. Within six months, Saoirse was a 24-year-old VP of Product Management.

3 Your key task: write up your role vision and anticipated priorities

It will be a more powerful pitch for the next role if you have a written document that describes your three-year vision for the role, your first 12-month priorities, and what you would do in your first 100 days plan to get off to an accelerated start.

YOUR NEXT ROLE	
Role Vision Envisage a three-year role horizon	What I want to achieve within three years in this role on: – Strategy – People & Teams – Results & Deliverables
12-Month Priorities Given what you want to achieve within three years, what are your priorities for the first 12 months?	Critical business areas for first 12 months:
First 100 Days Plan Now, with that context in mind, write your First 100 Days Plan	My top 10 desired outcomes by end of First 100 Days:

10

Close the deal

- Execute your get-promoted plan
- Be ready to negotiate: a promotion without a pay rise is not a promotion
- What to do if they refuse to promote you
- You got the promotion … now what?! The importance of your First 100 Days

1 Execute your get-promoted plan

do something and something will happen

Let's pull it all together, and create your get-promoted action plan. Do something and something will happen. Do nothing and nothing will happen.

Let's review all 7 Ps and the associated insights and key tasks, so that you can have a complete review of all the insights and learnings on offer and decide what you specifically need to do next. You should set a date for completing your key tasks. Depending on what resonated with you, feel free to calibrate your actions per P accordingly – but don't ignore any of the essential 7 Ps. If there is one P that makes you particularly uncomfortable, then pay even closer attention to completing the key task associated with that P.

Table 10.1 Your get-promoted plan

THE 7 PS	INSIGHTS/TOPICS	KEY TASK	BY WHEN
Purpose: Why do you want the promotion?	Set out a vision for your career. Promotion is about a path to leadership.	Develop your career game plan	
emPower yourself: Take charge of your career	Take back control. Create, don't wait.	Make a list of empowering strategies	
Personal impact: Be confident about your ability to step up	Appreciate the experience you would bring. Tame your inner critic.	Develop your value proposition for promotion	
Politics: Stack the odds in your favour	Learn how to read the organisation. Build influence and leverage.	Understand the politics of your promotion	

THE 7 PS	INSIGHTS/TOPICS	KEY TASK	BY WHEN
People: Figure out who really makes the decision	Identify the decision-makers and the influencers. Launch your campaign.	Map the critical stakeholders	
Performance: Deliver great results to get attention	Establish an impressive platform of results. Identify the next big wave.	Shape new ideas	
Proactivity: Put yourself forward for the role	When and how to ask for promotion. If at first you don't succeed, ask again.	Develop your role manifesto – 3-year vision, 12-month priorities, First 100 Days Plan	

Having familiarised yourself with the content of this book, and having set out your plan, remember that a key next step will be to ASK FOR YOUR PROMOTION.

Advice from the top

I learned early on that you don't just get rewarded with a promotion for knuckling down and executing. There's so much more on top of it. It takes time and you've got to plan and build that plan into your development as you progress as a leader. The key elements are visibility, networking and building your profile both internally and externally in a very positive way. All of this needs to be done on the back of what you are trying to execute in your business. People need to understand what you are doing and the value you are driving for the business. There's a technique to getting promoted. It doesn't happen by accident or by fate. You need to understand how to drive your visibility, your development and ultimately your promotion. And you need to build the competency to do all three, and you have to plan all of this.

DARREN PRICE, GROUP CHIEF INFORMATION
OFFICER AND EXECUTIVE BOARD MEMBER,
RSA INSURANCE GROUP

Have a plan. And once you've decided what you want, it's about relentless pursuit and about respecting people both above and below you on the career scale. My plan revolved around improving the level of education I had, putting myself in the right situations within organisations, and while never neglecting what I was supposed to do on a day-to-day basis, start assuming some of the responsibilities of the role that I wanted. Very often leaders are happy to delegate responsibility and by showing capability to do those things, you're demonstrating the ability to operate at the next level. Take your opportunities – look for the openings and make sure that people know that you want them. Think of the best salesperson in the world – if they are going to close a sale, they will ask the customer for the order. It is such a simple thing, but make sure that people know you are ambitious by asking them for what you want, and make sure that you have the track record to say this is what I've achieved, and this is why I'm suitable.

JOHN QUINN, GROUP CHIEF TECHNOLOGY
OFFICER, DIGICEL

> *First, focus on the 'headache' areas for your organisation and your boss ... In my experience, the greatest development comes hand in hand with the most impactful projects, allowing you to make a real difference to your organisation while providing you with the important stretch and exposure. Second, have a plan in mind. Where do you want to be eventually? 'Start with the end in mind': focus on this and then work back on the development steps you need to get there. This can involve taking on another role or responsibilities outside of your comfort zone to get the experience. Third, positively volunteer for everything ... you will surprise yourself with your own resourcefulness and how this positivity will open doors for you.*
>
> CARL FITZSIMONS, GROUP HUMAN
> RESOURCES DIRECTOR, MW BRANDS

2 Be ready to negotiate: a promotion without a pay rise is not a promotion

Your goal is to get promoted, but let's be very clear about what that means. If a pay rise does not accompany your new title, or new set of responsibilities, then you have not secured a promotion. If your career game plan means you have deliberately chosen a lateral move, to reposition for a future promotion, then that is fine. Or you may even be okay with a step back, if it means you join a bigger-brand company, in service of a longer-term strategy for your career. As long as you are in charge of your move, and the rationale behind it, then

as long as you are in charge of your move, and the rationale behind it, then do what you want

do what you want. But if you wanted a promotion, and you got everything you wanted except the accompanying pay rise, then you did not get a real promotion – and don't let anyone try to tell you otherwise.

Unfortunately some bosses can be quite manipulative and they will exploit your desire to get ahead by telling you they are giving you a promotion – and get you all excited – but later say that there is no money in the budget for a pay rise. They use a context like cost-cutting and economic downturn to explain, and they try to spin it that at least you will get a better title, more experience and a chance of greater promotion prospects in the future.

Perhaps even more tricky is when you get a promotion, but the subsequent package on offer from HR is lower than what you expected. Your boss might choose not to fight your corner with HR and you won't want to be seen as ungrateful or greedy. You might even feel that you would jeopardise your chances by speaking up. Again this can feel very unfair to you. But this is one of those situations where your amount of leverage comes into play. If it is a step-up promotion – and the organisation is investing in the possibility that you will be a success – then perhaps you wait for next year's performance appraisal to renegotiate your terms. By then, you will have proved yourself. Alternatively if you feel you have a lot of leverage because you have a great case for why they need you, or you have other role options that you are willing to exercise, then you are in a much stronger position to negotiate better terms now. Initially you may have to stomach a low pay rise, but once in role and over time the power will shift back to you and that's when you should nail the right remuneration package.

Although the decision-maker and HR appear to have more power than you, don't give it all away. You need to be ready to anticipate, counteract and negotiate the terms of your promotion. The way to do this is to expect the possibility of a low – or no – pay rise in advance, and be ready to stand up for yourself. One way to do this early on is to clearly define what you mean by a promotion when you first ask for it. In other words, when you ask for promotion, explain in full that what you mean is 'a promotion with an accompanying pay rise'.

- Be ready to negotiate
    - Use facts, not emotions, to explain your case
    - Use any leverage at your disposal

- Look at the full reward package. Perhaps if one area is not negotiable, you can get more upside in another aspect:
    - salary
    - job title
    - office or desk location
    - paid time off
    - perks (e.g. leadership development courses).

3 What to do if they refuse to promote you

If you feel as if you have put the required effort into getting promoted, and that you are no further forward in terms of the commitment from your boss or your part of the organisation to invest in you, then you will need to change your environment. This may mean an internal move from the front line to a head office role, or you switch company divisions, or you move geographical location. Essentially you need to find a better boss and a new environment where you feel you can really flourish. It could also mean changing companies. But even if you feel disgruntled in your current company, you need to carefully weigh up the risks and benefits of joining a new company. There are risks inherent in moving to a company where you have no track record. You don't fully understand the culture or the politics and it can feel like starting all over again in terms of building up a reputation and forging bonds with new stakeholders – but, as a major upside, it can also represent an opportunity for a fresh start. If you feel you can create a better future in the new company then this is the ultimate decider. Make sure you wait until you have signed the job contract for the new company before you hand in your resignation.

Of course you don't need to be disgruntled to consider moving to a new company. It may be that you get a job offer you can't refuse. Or perhaps your career game plan requires you to get the kind of experience that only your new company can provide. Think about what you would be giving up. Think about what you would be gaining. The more senior you are, the more risk you are taking by joining a new company – because you have no experience yet of how its politics work. Take into account the risk that if it doesn't work out, you may be bounced out of that organisation within two years. Do you have a contingency plan if that happened?

do you have a contingency plan?

Table 10.2 Major risks and benefits of joining a new company

MAJOR RISKS OF JOINING A NEW COMPANY	MAJOR BENEFITS OF JOINING A NEW COMPANY
No reservoir of goodwill.	Opportunity for a fresh start.
No streetwise knowledge of the culture or the politics.	Likely bigger pay and reward package to compensate you for making the move.
Your key sponsor may not provide adequate air cover or leaves before you are successfully integrated.	Joining a new company gives you an opportunity for a new beginning and opens up new possibilities. It may re-energise you and rejuvenate your career. A major change represents a major growth opportunity.
In your current company, you are able to rely on your track record and years of relationship goodwill built up with others to get things done. In a new company, no matter how senior and experienced you are, you might find it difficult to get things done in a new culture.	

Case example

DAVID AND WHY HE LEFT AND THEN RE-JOINED HIS COMPANY

David worked at a large multinational technology company for over 10 years, working in four Senior Manager positions in sales and marketing. The opportunity to step up to Director level never seemed to come his way. Fed up with his situation, David began to apply for some roles outside the company. He was offered a Senior Manager role in a much smaller company for more pay, and took the job.

Within weeks of joining the new company, David could see a number of ways to improve how business was operating. Some of the processes in place were ineffective to the point of costing the company time and money. He went to his line manager – the Executive VP of Marketing – and discussed how streamlining these processes would have a huge impact on the business. Having come from a much larger company, David was used to really fighting his corner and he supported his argument with a strong business case and an abundance of evidence. David's boss immediately saw value in the proposal and said, *'Great, let's take this to the CEO and leadership team now.'*

David was shocked. In his old job, it took months to get access to the *real* decision-makers and even with a strong proposal such as his, it would have been a political struggle to drive change and secure buy-in from all parties. David and his boss presented the new processes to the CEO and the leadership team and immediately gained their support. David was surprised by how *easy* it had been. Sure, it was a smaller company with a flatter structure. But the reality was simple: by demonstrating value to the business with the support of the *right*

▶

advocate, he got access to the leadership team and won them over. Within eight months in the company, David was a trusted adviser for both the CEO and his team, and was promoted to a Senior Director role in the company.

Several years later (and an Executive Vice President role in another small company), David heard about a Director role in his previous company – the bigger-brand multinational. When he left the company five years previously David had had no intention of returning. Despite this, he had made a conscious effort to leave the business on very good terms. He left a comprehensive handover plan for his replacement and wrote personal notes to the executives and colleagues that he worked with over the years, thanking them for all they had done.

David got in touch with a few of his former colleagues to find out who the hiring Manager was. The hiring Manager was a senior figure who had been at the company when he was there before, but whom he had never met. He reached out to her via his network to tell her that he was interested in the job. He outlined why he would be suitable for the role and asked if she thought he should apply. She called him to come in for a chat. David was greeted warmly – she had enquired about David and had heard great things about him. With his 'small company' Director and VP level experience over the previous years and a solid reputation, David was re-hired as a 'big company' Director.

Reflecting on his journey, David wondered if he had ever needed to leave. Yes, he gained considerable experience by joining a new company and it's certainly true that large companies can be much slower to promote, with more competition for promotion. But what if he had just gone directly to the General Manager when he was at the multinational and had told him he wanted more meaningful projects and opportunities to show his strategic value and to justify the promotion?

4 You got the promotion ... now what?! The importance of your first 100 days

Congratulations on getting your promotion! Now think about how to have a positive start in your new role. Your first 100 days set the tone for the rest of your role tenure. It is an opportunity to reset and renew who you are as a leader. It may mark the end of all your efforts to get promoted, but it is in fact a new beginning. It is the beginning phase of what will ultimately become your new role legacy, and a good start bodes well.

your first 100 days set the tone for the rest of your role tenure

The following is an excerpt from my book *Your First 100 Days: how to make maximum impact in your new leadership role*, published by Pearson in 2011.

WILL I SUCCEED OR FAIL?

Role beginnings bring a heady mix of excitement, anticipation and nervousness too. There is a feeling of being the 'special one' – singled out from others to be promoted and take on an important role.

However, there is also a feeling of trepidation – am I really good enough? Will I succeed or fail?

Leaders, however experienced, are emotional beings just like everybody else. In my experience, everybody who is facing into their first 100 days oscillates between these feelings of 'special one'/'superiority and 'worried one'/inferiority. Regulating your emotions during the beginning stage of your first 100 days is an important key to your success. At the beginning of an important role appointment, some executives feel overwhelmed by a feeling of panic and fear of failure. Others are over-confident and completely underestimate the challenges ahead. Try to stay centred from the beginning. If you can stay grounded, and can feel calm and confident in yourself from the beginning, you are giving yourself a chance to make the best possible start in the role.

It might seem like an odd thing, especially to junior people who think their leaders always know what to do, but I have noticed that very often senior executives simply don't know how to get started properly in a new role. After all, there is so much to do – sometimes it can be very difficult to know how to take that first step and start. The temptation is there to simply dive in and tackle the first problem that presents itself, and then the next and the next. This approach of 'getting stuck in' is their answer on how to start. It's one way, but it is way too reactive and it is certainly not the most thoughtful or strategic way to tackle a new role appointment.

THE IMPORTANCE OF YOUR FIRST 100 DAYS

The importance of your first 100 days is the difference between success and failure in this new role – and that has consequences for your whole career.

If you have a successful first 100 days, it naturally follows that you are setting yourself up for a successful first 12 months in this role. You will want to succeed in this role for its own sake – because this is your new promotion and this is the job that you are being asked to do. But look at the bigger picture too. If you get this role right, if you succeed in this role better and faster than expected, then it naturally follows that you are more likely to get promoted sooner to an even better role, even faster, and you can continue to enjoy accelerated success in your career ambitions.

Get it right from the beginning and you will get promoted faster into your next role. The opposite is also true. If you get off to a slow start, or a 'no-start', then imagine how much more difficult it will be to claw back lost time in an attempt to succeed later. If you fail to get it right from the beginning, then you seriously risk success in this role which can stall or reduce your future career prospects. After all, if you cannot succeed in this role, then why offer you another promotion? Seen in the context of the bigger picture of your career, the importance of your first 100 days in a senior role appointment cannot be underestimated.

FIRST 100 DAYS TRANSITION CHALLENGES: COMMON PITFALLS AND DERAILERS

The primary task for the newly appointed leader desiring first 100 days success is to set out the right strategic priorities and stay focused on them. In my specialist work as First100 founder and adviser, I identify a list of common challenges inherent in every transition that will affect the newly appointed leader. These can derail good intentions and get in the way of successfully achieving that primary task.

FIRST 100 DAYS CHALLENGES	
● Time pressures and intense learning curve	It takes time to get up to speed on the content of your new position, and yet business and markets cannot slow down and wait for you to catch up. Decisions still need to be taken and consequently the pressure can build up and will need to be managed in order to stay operating effectively.
● Being overwhelmed with immediate 'fire-fighting' and task-driven priorities	It would be tempting to 'get busy' and dive into the immediate business tasks and issues. But you need to have the strength of character to step back, and take time out to look at the big picture: what tasks should you continue, what should you stop, and what should you start?

FIRST 100 DAYS CHALLENGES

● Need to invest energy in building new networks and forging new stakeholder relationships	There is no point in having the right vision and strategy in isolation of bringing people with you. The culture may be dense and slow moving – people may be resistant to the changes you bring. Invest early in the influencer and stakeholder network.
● Dealing with legacy issues from your predecessor	Depending on the quality of your predecessor, your unit may or may not have a good reputation, and your team may have developed poor habits, behaviours and disciplines that will take time to address. Or you may have to endure the scenario of filling the shoes of a much-loved predecessor and being resented as the new guy whose mandate is to change how things have always been done before.
● Challenges on inheriting or building a team and having to make tough personnel decisions	Don't expect underperformers to have been weeded out prior to your arrival. A key task in your first 100 days will be to assess the quality of your team: who stays, who goes, and who else is needed onboard. And unfortunately, your best performer is probably now de-motivated and resentful – and consequently underperforming – because he applied unsuccessfully for your job.
● For external appointees: a lack of experience of new company culture may lead to inadvertent gaffes and early political blunders – all of which can take time to recover	From the innocuous to the significant, everything you do is being judged as indicative of your character. Merely checking your smart phone during a meeting may deeply offend your new role stakeholders who may judge that action as an indication that you are brash, disinterested and arrogant. You will need to be on 'hyper alert' to consciously pick up clues on the acceptable norms and behaviours.

FIRST 100 DAYS CHALLENGES	
● Getting the balance right between moving too fast and moving too slowly	New appointees sometimes panic and this can result in either doing too much (scatter gun approach, but not tackling the core issues) or doing too little ('I'll just listen for the first 3 months, and then decide what to do'). Neither extreme cuts it. Find the right balance.

It may seem unfair to present you with a list of new challenges when all you want to do is celebrate your success in getting the promotion. Yes, celebrate your achievement, and take a well-earned break before you start your new role. But then settle down and take the time to prepare yourself for success in the new role. By getting it right from the start of your new role, you are more likely to be promoted again – and faster!

I authored two books on the topic: *Your First 100 Days: How to make maximum impact in your new leadership role* (published by FT Publishing, 2011) and *Lead Your Team in your First 100 days* (published by FT Publishing, 2013), so these are available for you to consult. I go in depth into the insights on how to get off to an accelerated start in your new role, to set you up for success in your first 12 months and beyond. In particular I am keen that you take notice of the First100assist™ Framework which offers an expert perspective on how to write your First 100 Days Plan.

Final words

Dear Reader,

When I write my books I think deeply about the reader and really care about your success. With this topic of how to get promoted, I have tried to examine every possible angle in my attempt to help you. I hope you found it useful – and I hope you soon get the promotion you desire!

Please share your feedback and stories with me at niamh .okeeffe@CEOassist.com

Wishing you all the very best for a successful future,

Niamh

What did you think of this book?

We're really keen to hear from you about this book, so that we can make our publishing even better.

Please log on to the following website and leave us your feedback.

It will only take a few minutes and your thoughts are invaluable to us.

www.pearsoned.co.uk/bookfeedback

Index

Also by Niamh O'Keeffe

'An insightful 100 minutes read for
a great First 100 Days.'

Sander van't Noordende, Group Chief Executive
of Management Consulting, Accenture

Paperback and eBook available to buy now

Also by Niamh O'Keeffe

Paperback and eBook available to buy now

 FTPublishing   @FTPH